A GIRL CALLED JACK

A GIRL CALLED JACK

100 DELICIOUS BUDGET RECIPES

JACK MONROE

Photography by Susan Bell

MICHAEL JOSEPH
an imprint of
PENGUIN BOOKS

MICHAEL JOSEPH

Published by the Penguin Group

Penguin Books Ltd, 80 Strand, London WC2R 0RL, England

Penguin Group (USA) Inc., 375 Hudson Street, New York, New York 10014, USA

Penguin Group (Canada), 90 Eglinton Avenue East, Suite 700, Toronto, Ontario, Canada M4P 2Y3
(a division of Pearson Penguin Canada Inc.)

Penguin Ireland, 25 St Stephen's Green, Dublin 2, Ireland (a division of Penguin Books Ltd)

Penguin Group (Australia), 707 Collins Street, Melbourne, Victoria 3008, Australia
(a division of Pearson Australia Group Pty Ltd)

Penguin Books India Pvt Ltd, 11 Community Centre,

Panchsheel Park, New Delhi – 110 017, India

Penguin Group (NZ), 67 Apollo Drive, Rosedale, North Shore 0632,
New Zealand (a division of Pearson New Zealand Ltd)

Penguin Books (South Africa) (Pty) Ltd, Block D, Rosebank Office Park,
181 Jan Smuts Avenue, Parktown North, Gauteng 2193, South Africa

Penguin Books Ltd, Registered Offices: 80 Strand, London WC2R 0RL, England

www.penguin.com

First published 2014
003

Text copyright © Jack Monroe, 2014
Photographs copyright © Susan Bell, 2014

The moral right of the copyright holders has been asserted

www.agirlcalledjack.com

Set in Arial
Colour reproduction by Altaimage, London
Printed and bound in Italy by Printer Trento Srl

A CIP catalogue record for this book is available from the British Library

ISBN: 978–0–718–17894–9

MIX
Paper from
responsible sources
FSC
www.fsc.org   FSC™ C018179

Penguin Books is committed to a sustainable
future for our business, our readers and
our planet. This book is made from Forest
Stewardship Council™ certified paper.

CONTENTS

Introduction 9
Hunger Hurts 12
Kitchen Essentials 14
Change Your Shopping Habits 18

1. Bread and Breakfast 20

2. Super Soups 40

3. Beans, Pulses and Lentils 60

4. Take a Packet of Pasta…80

5. Or a Bag of Rice…100

6. Vegetable Dishes 112

7. Fishes 138

8. Birds 156

9. Piggy 168

10. Sweets and Treats 188

And Another Thing … 208
Hunger Hurts – One Year Later 214
Index 216
Acknowledgements 222

'MY SON, WHOM I LOVE;

WITH HIM I AM WELL PLEASED.'

MATTHEW 3:17

INTRODUCTION

When I started writing my A Girl Called Jack blog back in February 2012, it was a local political commentary blog, reporting on Southend council meetings and local events. I didn't set out to write a food blog, nor a guide to life, and although the old adage says that 'everybody has a book inside them' I didn't imagine for one moment that I did, or that anyone would be interested in what I had to say.

When I started posting recipes online, they were an aside, cobbled together from ingredients in the value range at my local supermarket and cooked in a kitchen so small that I could touch both walls if I stood in the middle of it. I'd worked out that I could make a protein-packed tomato and bean soup for less money than the cheapest can of dubious 'tomato' soup in the supermarket, and I wanted to let people know, so they could perhaps eat a little better, for a little less.

With my tiny kitchen, a tiny budget and a tiny boy's mouth to feed on a daily basis, I grew herbs on my windowsill, nursing coriander, rosemary, parsley, thyme and mint, wedged in rusty loaf tins, where they toppled off when I turned the tap on in my sink to do the washing-up.

I had fantastic Home Economics teachers at school – Ms Farquhar, Miss Saville, Ms Kadic and Sheila, I salute you. I left secondary school with four and a half GCSEs, but with a gentle confidence that I knew my way around a carton of chopped tomatoes, and when I moved out of my parents' home seven years ago I started to explore, create, knead, taste, season and freeze, and scrabble in the back of the cupboard the week before pay day to find a bag of lentils, knowing I had to make dinner somehow. I kept black scribbled notebooks of my recipes, a standing joke among my friends – if something goes down well, they tell me to 'put it in the book' while the ingredients are still strewn around the kitchen.

I spent a year unemployed from 2011 to 2012, with a budget of around £10 per week for food for me and Small Boy. As terms like 'double-dip recession', 'austerity' and 'fiscal cliff' graced the news headlines and hit the wallets of the nations, I moved from shopping online and having swanky organic fruit and vegetables delivered in a recyclable cardboard box, to living out of the orange and white livery of the Basics range at my local supermarket. The ardent foodie in me was utterly miserable. Cheap, processed ready meals and a lack of fruit and vegetables led to poor sleep patterns and a constantly hungry child, and for the first time in my life my skin broke out in big angry spots. Something bad was going in, and nothing good was coming out of it.

Things had to change. I no longer had the well-stocked kitchen and ivory-coloured five-hob Rangemaster of my former home, nor the open-plan swank of the 'luxury executive apartment'; I had a kitchen I couldn't so much as lie down in, with an oven, a hob and two saucepans, but I decided to dust off my apron and cook meals from scratch, as cheaply as I possibly could. I cut down on meat and dairy products, out of necessity, and fell in love with home-cooked food again.

The results were, and continue to be, surprising. I found that my £10 weekly budget extended to home-baked breads for breakfast, thick wholesome protein-packed soups, warming winter casseroles and curries and stews, home-made burgers and piles of fruit and vegetables. Small Boy and I are healthier, happier and still a bit soft around the edges, with three meals a day and a supply of bread and snacks as and when we want them. Cooking for one and a half people used to feel pointless and laborious; now it's quick and delightful, with minimal preparation and washing-up. All my recipes can be made easily for one hungry person, or one person and a child, or in multiples thereof, and frozen for home-made ready meals.

Being a parent means I don't have hours to spend in the kitchen, so most of my recipes are speedy and simple. There's no tarting about, no fancy expensive ingredients, but still, when I call my friends and invite them over for dinner, I manage to fill a table and they manage to clear their plates with compliments and smiles and disbelief that I do it so cheaply.

I started to document my recipes on my online blog, www.agirlcalledjack.com, and soon different people were asking me every day if I would put them all into a cookbook. People emailed me to tell me how much money they were saving on their weekly shop, expressing surprise that their children were eating spicy tomato and haricot bean soup, or mushroom chasseur with piles of mash.

I don't claim to be the world's greatest cook, but I can sweat an onion and sauté a mushroom with the best of them; and in an age of glossy 'food porn' on our televisions watched while stabbing ready meals with a fork, there seems to be a disheartening disconnect between fantastic, nutritious food and the myth that one needs a fancy kitchen and seventy 'store cupboard essentials' to cook them with. It's simply not true. Cooking can be easy. And I believe that in order to tackle food poverty and a culture of microwave meals with dubious ingredients, cooking at home needs to be presented as less glossy, less sexy, less intimidating and more accessible, more about what you can make from what's in the cupboard, to spend less, reduce waste, and knock up a meal in ten minutes when you get home from work, or when you have a toddler tugging on your leg.

HUNGER HURTS

An excerpt from my blog in July 2012. The original title was 'Poverty isn't just having not enough food'. It has been read 20 million times, reblogged, retweeted, quoted in national newspapers, and I used it as my speech in Parliament last summer. This was the turning point.

Today has seen fourteen job applications go in, painstakingly typed on this Jurassic mobile phone, for care work, shop work, factory work, minimum-wage work, any kind of work, because quite simply, this doesn't work.

For reasons unbeknownst to me, this month my Housing Benefit was over £100 short. I didn't get a letter that I know of, but I can assume that it's still the fallout from the cockups made by the various benefit agencies when I briefly went back to work from March to May. Whatever the reason, it's easy to work out that £670 of rent can't be paid from £438 of Housing Benefit. So I'm a week in arrears, almost two, as by the time Thursday comes and the next £167.31 is due, there'll still be nothing coming in. The Income Support went on keeping me afloat, briefly, as did the Child Tax Credit. Now I'm not only in arrears, but last night when I opened my fridge to find some leftover tomato pasta, an onion and a knob of stem ginger, I gave the pasta to my boy and went to bed hungry with a pot of home-made ginger tea to ease the stomach pains.

This morning, Small Boy had one of the last Weetabix, mashed with water, with a glass of tap water to wash it down with. 'Where's Mummy's breakfast?' he asks, big blue eyes and two-year-old concern. I tell him I'm not hungry, but the rumblings of my stomach call me a liar. But these are the things that we do.

I sit at the breakfast table, pencil and paper in hand, and I start to make a list. Everything that I have was either given to me by benevolent and generous friends, or bought when I earned £27k a year and had that fuzzy memory of disposable income. Much of it has gone already. The Omega Seamaster watch, a 21st-birthday present, was the first to go when I left the Fire Service. My words 'you can't plead poverty with a bloody Omega on your bloody wrist' now ring true for most of my possessions as the roof over my head becomes untenable. My letting agents take care to remind me that I am on a rolling contract, and they can ask me to leave at any time, for no reason. I sell my iPhone for less than a quarter of its original price, and put my SIM in this Jurassic Nokia that I found in a drawer from days gone by.

Tomorrow, my small boy will be introduced to the world of pawnbroking, watching as his mother hands over the TV and the guitar for an insulting price, but something towards bridging the gap between the fear of homelessness, and hanging in for a week or two more. Trying to consolidate arrears, red-topped letters and bailiffs, with home security, is a day-to-day grind, stripping back further the things that I can call my own. Questioning how much I need a microwave. How much I need a TV. How much I need to have the fridge turned on at the mains. Not as much as I need a home, and more importantly, not as much as Small Boy needs a home.

People ask me how I can be so strong. People say to me that they admire my spirit. Days like today, sitting on my son's bed with a friend, numb and staring as I try to work out where the hell to go from here, I don't feel strong. I don't feel spirited. I just carry on.

First you turn your heating off. That was in December, it went off at the mains and I parked furniture in front of all the heaters to forget that they were ever there in the first place and alleviate the temptation to turn them on. Then you turn everything off at the wall sockets; nothing on standby, nothing leaking even pennies of electricity to keep the LCD display on the oven. Then you stop getting your hair cut; what used to be a monthly essential is suddenly a gross luxury, so you throw it back in an Alice band and tell your friends that you're growing it, not that you can't afford to get it cut. Everyday items are automatically replaced with the white and orange livery of Sainsbury's Basics, and everything is cleaned with 24p bleach diluted in spray bottles. You learn to go without things, and to put pride to one side when a friend invites you to the pub and you can't buy yourself a drink, let alone one for anyone else. There's a running joke that I owe a very big round when I'm finally successful with a job application, and I know I am lucky to have the friends that I do.

Then you start to take lightbulbs out. If they aren't there, you can't turn them on. Hallway, bedroom, Small Boy's bedroom, you deem them unnecessary, and then, in a cruel twist of fate, the E.ON man rings the doorbell to tell you that you owe £390, and that he's fitting a key meter, which will make your electricity more expensive to run. So you turn the hot water off. Cold showers were something of the norm in my old flat, where the boiler worked when it wanted to, so you go back to them.

You sell the meagre DVD collection for an even more meagre sum, the netbook, a camera; you wash clothes in basic washing powder that makes your skin itch. You pare back, until you have only two plates, two bowls, two mugs, two glasses, two forks, two knives, two spoons, because everything else feels like an indulgence, and rent arrears don't wait for indulgence.

In a world where people define other people by their job title (this is Sue, she's a lawyer, and Marcus, he's an architect) and by the number plate on the type of cars they drive, and the size of their television and whether it's 3D or HD or in every room, my world is defined by the love and generosity of my friends, and the contents of my bin shed. You sit on the sofa someone gave you, looking at the piano someone gave you, listening to the radio someone gave you, perched on the chest someone gave you.

Poverty isn't just having no heating, or not quite enough food, or unplugging your fridge and turning your hot water off. Poverty is the sinking feeling when your small boy finishes his one Weetabix and says, 'More, Mummy? Bread and jam please, Mummy,' as you're wondering whether to take the TV or the guitar to the pawn shop first, and how to tell him that there is no bread or jam.

KITCHEN ESSENTIALS

Store Cupboard Ingredients

I try to shop with the rules of a healthy balanced diet in mind, although it isn't always easy on a limited budget. I pick up my protein first, vegetables second, then buy 'one carb a week' – rotating through a bag of flour, a bag of rice, a packet of pasta and a few tins of potatoes. Finally, if there's anything left in the budget, I head back to the fruit aisle and then the tinned fruit department, to see what I can pick up. If you cook from this book for a week, you'll start to build up a store cupboard of ingredients that can be used again and again, making your food shop cheaper every time. But in order to start you off, here are a few essentials that I try to make sure I always have in the cupboard, and a few other hints and tips. Build up your cupboard contents over time – there's no rule that says you need to rush out and buy everything all at once.

Carbs – The cheapest rice in the shops is invariably white long grain rice, with brown varieties costing far more. The same goes for pasta. White flour is far cheaper than wholemeal flour – but I go by the principle of 'everything in moderation'. If you're cooking how I cook, with less fat, salt and sugar than you'll find in ready meals, then a little white pasta won't do you much harm! However, you can use any type of rice or pasta you like for my recipes, and wholemeal flour as a substitute for white.

Dairy – A large pot of plain natural yoghurt goes a long way, either as a standalone breakfast with some tinned fruit mixed in, or as a sauce in which to marinate chicken or toss with pasta with some lemon and herbs for a quick lunch. I also keep my eyes peeled for 'cheap cheese', my favourites being anything hard and strong or a value range Brie. Having some sort of cheese on standby is very useful – and the stronger the flavour, the less you need for a dish. Is it just me that doesn't understand the appeal of mild Cheddar?

Dark chocolate – Use as a base for Mexican soup and authentic chilli, or stir it melted into cornflakes to make cornflake cakes.

Fruit – Large bags of apples are good for kids' lunchboxes – or even your own – but fresh fruit can be expensive, so check out the tinned fruit too. Tins of peaches, pineapple chunks, broken mandarin segments and pears are all handy to have in the cupboard for stirring into yoghurt, tagines, curries or simply eating as a snack. The reduced chiller in the supermarket is your friend – if you find any punnets of berries or other small fruits here you can freeze them and store them for a few months.

Lemon juice – Bottled lemon juice is just as good as a bag of lemons and lasts longer.

Oil – Any oil will do. I use sunflower oil or vegetable oil for cooking. Olive oil is nice but ridiculously expensive in comparison, and I like the lightness of sunflower oil when making pestos and sauces, and the way that it takes on the flavour of the ingredients that it is mixed with. Olive oil also has a low burning point, so is unsuitable for frying or roasting.

Plain flour – Self-raising flour is great when you first open it, but the raising agents cease to be as effective once they come into contact with the air, so I just buy plain, and add 1 teaspoon of bicarbonate of soda or baking powder per 150g of flour. Flour is a useful staple for making bread and gnocchi, and for thickening sauces. People often express incredulity that I can make bread 'without bread flour' – but I can, and I do.

Protein – Many people associate protein with just meat and I've often been asked by readers where the protein in my diet comes from. Sources of protein are not limited to whole chickens and beef steaks, but can be found in much cheaper forms, such as tins of sardines, jars of fish paste and tins of beans and pulses. I eat meat around twice a week, fish twice a week, and vegetarian high-protein alternatives in between. I pack out soups with pulses and use them to make chilli, burgers, curry, as well as different flavourful stews. Beans, pulses and lentils are also a great source of fibre, and far cheaper and easier to store than a big joint of meat.

Raising agents – Bicarbonate of soda and dried yeast are essentials in my store cupboard, to knock up breads with. You can make a quick soda bread from just bicarb, flour, lemon juice and milk, so it's a good thing to have kicking about.

Spices – My essential spices are paprika, cumin and turmeric, and I use them liberally throughout my cooking to enliven simple ingredients. If you live near an Indian grocery store, buy them there in larger plastic bags as these are far cheaper than the small jars in the supermarket.

Stock cubes – I always have supermarket value range vegetable, chicken and beef stock cubes tucked away in the cupboard to use as a base for soups, sauces, gravy, curries and casseroles.

Tins – Tinned potatoes, tinned carrots, tinned kidney beans, tinned chopped tomatoes, tinned fish: tins are your friends. Tuck them in the cupboard, and you'll always have dinner on standby.

Vegetables – I buy most of my vegetables either frozen or tinned, or from the reduced chiller in the supermarket at the end of the evening. Large stew packs are useful for basic root vegetables, but they tend to be seasonal and unreliable – check your local shops to see what their ranges are. Tinned carrots, tomatoes and sweetcorn can often be cheaper than their fresh or frozen counterparts, and frozen spinach, peas and green beans are interchangeable in most recipes and handy to have on standby as a side dish or to bulk out meals. I buy onions in bulk, and keep them in the bottom drawer of the fridge – a large bag of onions will keep for around 3 weeks, and can be peeled, chopped and frozen to keep for longer (see Freezing Veg on page 210). Just break a chunk off when you want to use them. If you are fortunate enough to live near a good independent greengrocer, their fruit and vegetables may be cheaper than the local supermarket.

Wine – I buy a bottle of the supermarket's own red or white, although some stores now sell 'cooking wine' in small bottles, which is pretty much the same thing. I use wine in a lot of my cooking, especially casseroles, risottos and soups, where a little splash can make a big difference.

Hero Herbs

If you're starting a herb garden from scratch, start with just four plants: an 'everything' herb, a delicate herb, a woody herb and a chilli plant. I started out with coriander (my everything herb), mint (my delicate herb), thyme (my woody herb) and a chilli plant.

Everything herbs – Choose between parsley, a simple fresh herb that can be added to almost any dish, or coriander if you like curries and spicy food.

Delicate herbs – Mint and basil both have a fresh, uplifting flavour well suited to Mediterranean cooking, pasta dishes, light soups and home-made pestos.

Woody herbs – Start with thyme, rosemary or sage. Rosemary is very hardy but takes a little time to prepare. Sage is deliciously earthy and grows to fill the pot that it is in. Thyme does well on a sunny window ledge and can be plucked and snipped into tiny pieces.

Chillies – I've been growing tiny red chillies on a window ledge for years and I get a good crop all year round (I can harvest about a hundred in August when the plant is at its peak – see page 209 for how to preserve any surplus). Chilli plants can be bought very cheaply from the supermarket or garden centre and repay their cost very quickly.

Equipment

You don't need lots of gadgets and expensive equipment in order to cook from scratch – I often think that kitchens full of fancy whizzy gadgets leave no actual room on the work surface to chop, knead and generally make a mess. This is what I have in my kitchen, and it works for me.

Pans

1 large non-stick saucepan
1 smaller non-stick saucepan
1 large frying pan or sauté pan, with a lid

In the oven

1 roasting tin
1 baking sheet
1 loaf tin

In a drawer

2 wooden spoons
Masher
General cutlery
Sharp paring knife
Kitchen scissors
Small hand grater
Measuring jug or an old baby bottle

On the worktop

Blender – Mine is from the value range at the supermarket, cost about a tenner, and has been going for a few years now with heavy use. It blends on one setting or turns off, and that's all I need.

Scales – I only really use scales for measuring bread or cake ingredients, as everything else is a handful of this or whatever's left of that.

Large mixing bowl – I bought mine from the pound shop, a big metal bowl that is repurposed as a fruit bowl when not in use; slightly dented, but still a good mixing bowl.

And that's it. If you want to make life easier, you can get tongs for turning burgers instead of using a fork, and a garlic crusher – but they're a sod to clean. A few extra knives and spoons wouldn't go amiss, but they aren't essential when starting out. A vegetable peeler is useful for making courgette ribbons or carrot ribbons for pasta, but if you don't have one, grate the veg instead.

CHANGE YOUR SHOPPING HABITS

WRITE A LIST AND STICK TO IT It sounds obvious, but only deviate from the list to replace one item with a similar product for a similar price.

INVESTIGATE THE TINNED AISLE Tins are usually cheaper than fresh, whether fish, potatoes or fruit.

BUY FROZEN VEGETABLES You get more for your money, and if pre-sliced then someone's already done the hard work for you!

IGNORE FLASHY SIGNS IN THE SUPERMARKET Items on multi-buy deals are rarely nutritious and more likely to be biscuits and tins of sweets that weren't on your shopping list.

LOOK ON THE BOTTOM SHELVES FOR THE VALUE LABELS Items placed at eye level are often more expensive than those placed on the lower shelves or near the floor. Most everyday items can be found in a basic or value range: try tinned tomatoes, bags of apples, even fresh fish. Buy food for what's inside the packaging, not for the picture on the front.

'DOWNSHIFT' ONE BRAND AT A TIME If you normally buy premium brands, try the supermarket's own label version, and then try their basic brands – see if you can really tell the difference.

DON'T JUST GO TO THE SHOPS YOU ALREADY KNOW Corner shops can be full of bargains, like large bags of spices, and the local fruit and veg shop may be cheaper than the supermarket.

BUYING IN BULK DOESN'T ALWAYS MEAN CHEAPER Most shelf labels will give you the price per 100g as well as the packet price. If a big bag of pasta is 42p per 100g, but the value range is 10p per 100g, buy a few bags of the value range stuff, even if they're smaller packets.

DON'T WASTE FOOD A 'use by' date means that you need to consume that product by the date given or else it might go bad; a 'best before' date means the food is simply at its best before that date. Be wary of exceeding 'use by' dates – but 'best before' is just the manufacturer's opinion of when the food will be at its best. Check out www.approvedfood.co.uk for big discounts on food past its 'best before' date but which can still legally be sold.

WHAT'S IN YOUR STORE CUPBOARD? Check before you shop and plan what meals you can make from those ingredients – see the index at the back for ideas.

WRITE A MEAL PLAN BEFORE YOU GO SHOPPING By planning meals using similar ingredients you can spend less on a weekly shop than you normally would.

DON'T BE AFRAID TO SUBSTITUTE You can't go too far wrong using one green veg instead of another, or different herbs, or using a mixture of cumin and turmeric in all your curries and tagines.

GO MEAT-FREE TWO OR THREE DAYS A WEEK Meat is expensive, so have a good rifle through the many vegetarian recipes in this book for ideas – even the most hardened meat eater is unlikely to complain at a bowl of smoky rich bean chilli or a spicy vegetable curry.

TAKE A PEN OR CALCULATOR WITH YOU WHEN YOU SHOP My secret to shopping on a low budget is to keep track of costs all the way round the store, jotting down prices and adding up as I go. I take cash, not my card, and never spend more than I have in my hand.

BREAD AND BREAKFAST

How often are we told that breakfast is the most important meal of the day? And how many of us still skip it, or don't do it justice?

On weekdays, particularly with a Small Boy to organize in the mornings, I admit that breakfast for both of us is plain cereal or porridge oats with sultanas – but weekends are a time for pancakes, home-made breads and griddle scones. Making my own bread started with Soda Bread (see page 23), which has just four ingredients and requires no rising time. Then I went on from there to make other breads, adding whatever I had in the cupboard: tinned mandarins, chickpeas or herbs from the window.

All of the breads given in this chapter can be sliced and frozen, then toasted straight from the freezer as needed – but in my household home-made bread doesn't normally last that long!

SODA BREAD

So you think you can't make bread? Or that you need a fancy pants breadmaker to do so? RUBBISH! You have a natural, free breadmaker in your palms and your knuckles – and this easy recipe with no proving or rising time is a great place to start. A lot of soda bread recipes use wholemeal flour, salt and buttermilk or yoghurt – but true to my usual style, I've pared it back to the basics (although you can add 1 teaspoon of salt to the flour if you like). However, basic doesn't mean disappointing. This is gorgeous served warm with red fruit jam or butter, or dunked into hearty soups and stews. It goes without saying that it's one of my favourite and most tried-and-tested recipes, doesn't it?

Makes 1 small loaf

juice of ½ a lemon or 2 teaspoons bottled lemon juice

300ml semi-skimmed milk

400g self-raising flour (or 400g plain flour plus 2 heaped teaspoons baking powder or bicarbonate of soda), plus extra to shape the dough and dust the loaf

1½ level teaspoons bicarbonate of soda

Preheat the oven to 180°C/350°F/gas 4. Squeeze the lemon juice into the milk. Stand to one side for about 5 minutes to allow the liquid to curdle and separate.

Meanwhile, weigh the flour into a bowl, add the bicarbonate of soda and mix through. Make a well in the centre of the flour and pour in most of the milk-and-lemon mixture. Mix well with a wooden spoon to form a sticky dough. Use your judgement – if it looks too dry, add the remaining liquid.

Tip the dough on to a floured work surface and pat into a round shape, kneading ever so lightly. The trick to amazingly light soda bread is not to fiddle with it too much.

Pop the shaped dough into a 1lb loaf tin (approximately 17 x 7 x 6cm), score a line on top of the dough down the middle about 1cm deep with a sharp knife and dust with a little extra flour. Place in the preheated oven for 40 minutes. Once baked through, the loaf should sound hollow on the bottom when tapped and feel ridiculously light. Remove the tin from the oven, tip out the soda bread whilst hot and leave to cool on a wire rack.

Break into chunks and serve warm with butter, or allow to cool completely then wrap in cling film to keep fresh.

TIPS: Add a fistful of sultanas or other dried fruits to the dry ingredients before adding the liquid, shape the dough into 8 balls instead of one loaf and pop the balls into lightly oiled muffin tins or on to an oiled baking sheet to make soda bread muffin-scones. Adjust the cooking time accordingly – around 12 to 15 minutes should be fine. Halve the muffin-scones while warm, and serve with a dollop of red jam.

Soda bread goes stale very quickly, but if that happens don't throw it away! Day-old soda bread can still be sliced and toasted, served with butter or jam. Or use leftover soda bread to make Panzanella (see page 135).

CRACKERBREAD

Traditional bread made from just flour and water is more commonly known as unleavened bread – meaning that it is prepared and cooked without any raising agent such as yeast or, in the case of soda bread, bicarbonate of soda. Unleavened breads tend to be flat, due to the lack of raising agent, but not all flat breads are unleavened. Types of unleavened bread include matzo bread, eaten during Jewish Passover, as well as Mexican tortillas and Indian roti breads and chapattis. The recipe below makes crackers similar to matzo bread, which are delicious topped with jam as a snack for a small boy. I swear by having a bag of flour in the cupboard at all times, and this is one of the reasons why.

Makes 30 crackers

375g (3 cups) plain flour, plus extra to knead the dough

1 teaspoon salt

235ml (1 cup) water

Preheat the oven to 180°C/350°F/gas 4.

Place the flour and salt in a large mixing bowl. Make a well in the centre using either your hand or the back of a wooden spoon and carefully pour the water in. Combine the water with the flour quickly, using a wooden spoon.

When a sticky dough is formed, tip out on to a heavily floured work surface and knead for 10 minutes with your palms and knuckles. Break the dough into approximately 20 walnut-sized pieces. Roll each into a ball, flatten to a couple of millimetres thick with your palm or a rolling pin, and pierce lightly with a fork.

Place the flattened dough balls on a lightly greased baking tray and bake in the preheated oven for approximately 8 to 12 minutes, or until crisp around the edges. Remove from the oven and allow to cool on a wire rack before munching or storing.

SUNSHINE BREAD

The quantity given for the tin of pineapple chunks is approximate. Some tins are 200g, some are 227g, so don't worry about weighing and measuring – just throw about half the tin in! You can put the remaining pineapple chunks from the tin into an airtight container with just enough juice to cover and pop into the fridge to snack on or use in another recipe. For a portable breakfast for me and Small Boy, or as a snack to keep in my drawer to chipmunk away on in the busyness of my day, I like to make individual buns – see the tip below.

Makes 1 small loaf

350g plain flour, plus extra to knead the dough

a 7g sachet of fast-acting dried yeast

1 carrot

30g sultanas

½ x 200g tin of pineapple chunks and the juice from the whole tin

oil or butter, to grease the loaf tin

Weigh the flour into a large mixing bowl and add the yeast. Finely grate in the carrot and add the sultanas. Mix everything together, then make a well in the centre of the dry ingredients.

Strain the pineapple pieces over a measuring cup or bowl, reserving the juice to use in a minute. Tip the pineapple chunks into the centre of the dry mixture. Add lukewarm water to the pineapple juice to make it up to 160ml. Pour into the well in the centre of the ingredients on top of the pineapple chunks, and combine everything together to make a soft, sticky dough.

Tip the dough out on to a lightly floured work surface and knead lightly. As you knead it, the pineapple pieces may break down and make the dough wetter. If this happens, sprinkle some extra flour over the dough and knead it in. Leave to rise on the work surface for approximately 15 minutes.

Transfer the risen dough into a greased 1lb loaf tin (approximately 17 x 7 x 6cm), cover with cling film and leave to prove (the second rising process) for half an hour. A little before the end of the proving time, put on the oven to 180°C/350°F/ gas 4 to preheat.

Pop the loaf tin into the preheated oven for 45 minutes, until the bread is risen and crusty on top. It should feel light when you lift it from the oven and sound hollow when you tap the bottom. This is quite a moist bread, so can be left to cook a little longer if you prefer.

Allow to cool slightly, then tip out from the loaf tin. Slice, butter and eat.

TIPS: Sunshine bread is best eaten freshly cooked and warm, but if there is any left over for the next day simply lightly toast it to enjoy.

This recipe can also be made into Sunshine Buns, by shaping the dough into approximately 8 individual rounds or cutting into scone shapes with a large cookie cutter and putting into greased muffin tins. Reduce the baking time to around 18 minutes.

CHICKPEA AND TOMATO BEST BRUNCH LOAF

This loaf is a favourite weekend recipe of mine, which is easily adapted to personal tastes and what you have in the cupboard. Sometimes I like to thoroughly mash the chickpeas for a smoother bread, sometimes I chuck them in whole for a knobbly, crunchy texture.

Makes 1 small loaf

240g tinned chickpeas (drained weight)

300g plain white flour, plus extra to knead the dough

a 7g sachet of fast-acting dried yeast

a handful of chopped fresh rosemary

zest and juice of ½ a lemon or 1 tablespoon bottled lemon juice

1 large tomato, deseeded and chopped into small chunks

TIPS: Store the loaf for up to 3 days, wrapped in cling film to keep it fresh. If it starts to go stale, toast it and eat spread with butter.

For a delicious and filling dish, make the bread with 5 or 6 finely chopped sun-dried tomatoes in place of the fresh tomato and serve toasted with bacon and a poached egg on top.

Drain the chickpeas, thoroughly rinse and put into a large mixing bowl. Mash with a potato masher to loosen the skins and pick these off as the chickpeas separate (not an essential step but definitely worth it for the end result!)

Add the flour, yeast, chopped rosemary and finely grated lemon zest, if available, to the chickpeas and stir together with a wooden or silicone spoon. Then stir in the chopped tomato.

Squeeze the lemon juice into a measuring cup and add lukewarm water to make up to 160ml of liquid. Make a well in the middle of the chickpea and flour mixture and pour in half of the liquid, mixing together. Gradually add as much of the remaining liquid as you need until a soft, sticky dough is formed but which is firm enough to shape.

Lightly flour your work surface, then tip the dough out and knead and stretch it for 10 minutes. Pummel the dough, pound it, mush your knuckles into it – it's like a stress ball but much more satisfying! Pop the dough back into the mixing bowl, cover with a tea towel or cling film and leave to rise for 2 hours. This sounds like a long time but the end result is a gorgeous light loaf with a proper crust around it.

Knock back the risen dough, shape into a rugby ball shape and pop it into a lightly greased 1lb loaf tin (approximately 17 x 7 x 6cm), then cover and leave to prove for half an hour. A little before the end of the proving time, put on the oven to 220°C/425°F/gas 7 to preheat.

Put the tin into the preheated oven and cook for 30 minutes, until the bread is risen and golden. Remove the loaf from the tin and allow to cool on a wire rack.

CABBAGE GRIDDLE SCONES

Griddle scones can be a simple weekend breakfast to make those lazy Sunday mornings feel special and luxurious. Although these are extraordinarily easy to make, when I taste the sweet crunch of fried greens with melted butter or see a mixing bowl and spoon in the washing-up pile I feel like I've achieved something, even if it's almost midday. I like to eat my griddle scones warm straight from the pan with butter, natural yoghurt or a squeeze of lemon juice. To make a sweet version, simply substitute a handful of sultanas or other dried fruits for the cabbage and serve with red jam.

Makes 4 large scones

70g finely shredded cabbage or other leafy greens

200g self-raising flour (or 200g plain flour plus 1 heaped teaspoon baking powder or bicarbonate of soda), plus extra to knead the dough

1 level teaspoon bicarbonate of soda

optional: a pinch of salt

50ml milk or 2 tablespoons natural yoghurt and a splash of water

2 eggs

oil, to fry the scones

Toss the shredded cabbage or greens into a mixing bowl. Pour over the flour, add the bicarbonate of soda and salt, if using, and make a well in the centre of the dry ingredients.

Pour the milk, or yoghurt and water, into the well and break the eggs on top. Mix together with a wooden spoon until it forms a pliable – but not too sticky – dough. Briefly knead the dough on a heavily floured work surface, then flatten to around 2.5cm thick. Using a large cookie cutter (approximately 8cm), cut individual scones from the dough.

Heat a little oil in a frying pan and drop each round of dough in. You may need to cook them in batches. Fry on a medium heat for 2 minutes on each side, or until risen and golden. Repeat until all of the dough is used up. Serve warm.

TIPS: These are delicious with any soft cheese – such as goat's cheese, feta cheese or Brie – dolloped on top or with a hard cheese like Cheddar or Red Leicester grated into the mixture before cooking.

For a filling brunch, top with a couple of slices of fried bacon and a fried egg.

BEER AND SULTANA BREAD

This recipe uses only part of a can or bottle of bitter, but don't worry – pour the rest into a glass and pop it in the fridge to go flat, because you can make a Beery Berry Crumble (see page 205) out of that later. Waste not, want not! I use a cake tin to make this loaf in because I haven't got any baking trays for some bizarre reason, but that works really well in keeping the lovely 'round' shape. Serve the bread warm cut into chunks like a scone, with butter and plum, fig or your choice of jam. Mmm!

Makes 1 small loaf

200g plain flour, plus extra to knead the dough

a 7g sachet of fast-acting dried yeast

a small knob of fresh ginger, peeled, or a pinch of ground ginger

50g sultanas

160ml bitter

Weigh the flour into a large mixing bowl and add the yeast. Grate in the ginger, add the sultanas and mix through quickly with a fork or wooden spoon. Make a well in the centre of the flour mixture and add a generous splash of bitter. Mix the liquid into the flour and keep adding the bitter little by little until it forms a sticky dough.

Tip the dough on to a well-floured work surface and knead and stretch for 10 minutes. Form it into a rounded lump shape, then leave to rise for at least half an hour, uncovered.

Knock the excess air out of the risen dough – but keeping the rounded shape – and place in a lightly greased cake tin, Victoria sandwich tin or on a baking tray. Cover with cling film and leave the dough to rise in the tin for 1 to 2 hours until it's doubled in size. A little before the end of the proving time, put on the oven to 180°C/350°F/gas 4 to preheat.

Uncover the dough. Score the top with two lines each way like you're going to play noughts and crosses on it, and pop the tin into the middle of the preheated oven for 35 to 40 minutes.

Take the bread out of the oven, turn out of the tin and leave to cool on a wire rack. Then cut into thick slices and devour with butter. I start eating mine as soon as it's cool enough to touch!

TIPS: The best way to peel ginger is by scraping away the skin with a teaspoon.

Add a heaped tablespoon of oats to the flour and yeast mixture, and sprinkle some more on top of the dough before putting it into the oven.

Use finely chopped fresh plums or dried prunes instead of the sultanas.

VEGAN BANANA BREAD

Use a mild-flavoured oil such as vegetable or sunflower oil for this recipe – I would not recommend olive oil, which overpowers the other ingredients. This bread is absolutely delicious the next day, toasted under a grill and buttered – or with peanut butter for a seriously indulgent treat!

Makes 1 small loaf

3 large ripe bananas

75ml vegetable or sunflower oil, plus extra to grease the loaf tin

50g sugar, or more to taste

225g self-raising flour (or 225g plain flour and 1 heaped teaspoon baking powder or bicarbonate of soda)

2 level teaspoons baking powder or 1 level teaspoon bicarbonate of soda

2 teaspoons ground cinnamon

optional: a generous handful of sultanas or mixed dried fruit

Preheat the oven to 180°C/350°F/gas 4 and lightly grease a 1lb loaf tin (approximately 17 x 7 x 6cm).

Peel the bananas, slice and mash with a fork in a large mixing bowl. If the bananas aren't the old, squishy sort, add a little of the oil to soften them and start them off. Add the rest of the oil and the sugar to the bowl, and mix well. It will look revolting but don't worry – it's perfectly normal and it gets better. Then tip in the flour, baking powder, cinnamon and sultanas (if you are using them), and stir well with a spoon to form a lumpy batter.

Pour the mixture into the prepared loaf tin and bake for 1 hour in the centre of the preheated oven, until the loaf has risen and is golden. If a knife or skewer inserted into the middle comes out clean, then it's done.

Remove the tin from the oven and allow to cool on a wire rack before turning out and slicing.

TIPS: If you don't want to use a full hour's worth of gas or electricity, make individual banana bread muffins. Lightly grease the cups of a muffin tin and spoon the mixture in until each cup is two-thirds full. I don't bother with paper cases at all – the muffins freeze better without them, and you get more of the crisp, crusty edge. Cook fairy cake-sized ones for 12 minutes, or larger muffins for 15 to 20 minutes, until they are risen and golden.

This loaf keeps really well for a few days. Just toast a slice to refresh it.

To make 8 chunky vegan banana sultana pancakes, mix together 2 mashed bananas, 100g self-raising flour, 100ml soya milk and a handful of sultanas to form a smooth batter. Heat 2 tablespoons of oil in a frying pan on a medium heat and fry the batter 1 tablespoon at a time, for 1 to 2 minutes on each side, then serve the pancakes in stacks with lemon, sugar, honey or warmed peanut butter on top. For a non-vegan version, use normal dairy milk and substitute a beaten egg for 1 of the mashed bananas.

COURGETTE, SULTANA AND LEMON BREAD

Courgettes give off quite a bit of liquid when you grate them but don't worry about draining it off in this recipe because the courgettey water will help to flavour the bread and add moisture. When you will be adding water to a recipe later anyway, it doesn't make sense to fanny about taking liquid out only to put it back in again, and I like simple solutions. I often start preparing my bread last thing at night so I can take the frustrations of the day out on it as I knead, which gives the additional bonus of being able to leave the dough overnight to rise for extra light and fluffy bread. This bread is delicious sliced and toasted with butter (or whatever spread you have) and marmalade, or simply eaten warm by the handful.

Makes 1 small loaf

1 small courgette

300g plain flour, plus extra to knead the dough

a 7g sachet of fast-acting dried yeast

50g sultanas

zest and juice of ½ a lemon or 1 tablespoon bottled lemon juice

Grate the courgette finely into a large mixing bowl. Add the flour and yeast to the courgette, then tip in the sultanas. Combine everything with a wooden spoon, making sure the courgette doesn't all just clump together.

Pour the lemon juice into a measuring cup, grate in the zest and add lukewarm water to make it up to 150ml of liquid (less than usual for this amount of flour because of the wetness of the courgette). Make a well in the centre of the dry mixture and pour in most of the lemon-water. Mix to form a sticky dough, adding the rest of the liquid if required.

Tip the dough out on to a lightly floured work surface and knead for about 10 minutes. Leave the dough to rise for half an hour, with a tea towel over the top to keep the heat in.

When the dough has risen, knock the air out of it, and pop into a lightly oiled or silicone 1lb loaf tin (approximately 17 x 7 x 6cm). Cover with cling film and leave to rise again (this is called proving) for at least another half an hour or, if you're like me, overnight. A little before the end of the proving time, put on the oven to 180°C/350°F/gas 4 to preheat.

Score the top of the dough lightly. Put the tin into the preheated oven and bake for 35 minutes; the loaf should be golden and crisp on top, feel lightweight and sound hollow on the bottom when tapped. Take out of the oven, remove the loaf from the tin and leave to cool on a wire rack, then slice and devour.

MANDARIN AND POPPY SEED LOAF

I like to make this bread in the evening to wind down and de-stress. Kneading the dough for 10 minutes may sound like a long time but it's very therapeutic to do at the end of the day, and those 10 minutes will go faster than you think! This recipe uses half the mandarin segments from a standard 300g (or thereabouts) sized tin. You can keep the remaining half of the fruit in an airtight container in the fridge to use another day.

Makes 1 small loaf

½ x 300g tin mandarin segments in juice and the juice from the whole tin

300g plain flour, plus extra to knead the dough

a 7g sachet of fast-acting dried yeast

1 tablespoon poppy seeds

oil to grease the bowl and loaf tin

optional: extra flour to top the loaf

TIPS: This loaf will keep for 3 days in an airtight container or for a month if frozen. I wrap mine in cling film once it has cooled and it's still absolutely fresh and delicious the day after.

Shape the dough into 12 small balls instead of one loaf and pop the balls into lightly oiled muffin tins to make scones. Adjust the cooking time accordingly, depending on the size of the muffin tins – around 12 to 15 minutes should be fine.

Drain the mandarin segments and reserve the juice in a measuring cup. Chop the segments into 1cm pieces. (I put them in a mixing bowl and attack with kitchen scissors, rather than messing about slipping all over a work surface.) Add the flour, yeast and poppy seeds to the bowl and combine.

Add lukewarm water to the reserved mandarin juice to make up 160ml of liquid. Make a well in the centre of the dry ingredients and add the liquid gradually, working the mixture in with a wooden spoon. Continue until you have a slightly sticky dough. Lightly flour your work surface and tip the dough on to it. Knead and stretch the dough for about 10 minutes.

Lightly oil the inside of the bowl, put the dough back into it, cover with a clean tea towel and leave to rise until doubled in size. This takes about half an hour, but the time varies depending on the temperature of the room.

When the dough has risen, knock the air out by tipping it back on to a lightly floured work surface and gently shaping into a rugby ball shape. Lightly oil a 1lb loaf tin (approximately 17 x 7 x 6cm), then lovingly place your rugby ball of goodness in it, pop the tea towel back on top and leave for another half an hour. This process is called proving.

A little before the end of the proving time, put on the oven to 220°C/425°F/gas 7 to preheat. Score the top of the loaf, sprinkle over some extra flour on the top for a rustic look and pop the tin into the preheated oven for 30 minutes. When it's done the loaf should sound hollow on the bottom when tapped.

Remove the tin from the oven, tip out the loaf and allow to cool on a wire rack. Then slice and eat!

GARLIC, HERB AND LEMON BREAD

If you want to be really traditional and a little bit messy, you can get stuck in and use your hands to mix together the ingredients and form the dough. You need a good swirling motion, but I've made a lot of bread and never quite got this right. It's good for the homespun warm feeling, not so great when you try to get out the little remnants of dough from under your fingernails and in the creases of your knuckles afterwards!

Makes 1 small loaf

250g plain white flour, plus extra to knead the dough

a 7g sachet of fast-acting dried yeast

2 cloves of garlic

2 handfuls of fresh parsley

zest and juice of 1 lemon or 2 tablespoons bottled lemon juice

1 tablespoon vegetable oil, plus extra to grease the bowl and loaf tin

TIPS: If doubling the quantities to make a 2lb loaf, the timing will be slightly different. After the first 15 minutes turn the oven down to 170°C/325°F/gas 3 and allow to cook for another 30 minutes.

Will keep for 3 days in an airtight container, or 1 month if frozen.

Put the flour and yeast into a large mixing bowl. Peel the garlic cloves and finely chop or crush. Finely chop the parsley into a small bowl or tea cup using kitchen scissors. Grate the lemon zest. Add the garlic, parsley and lemon zest to the flour and yeast with a flourish and stir to mix.

Measure the lemon juice into a measuring cup and add the oil. Pour in lukewarm water to make up to 180ml. Make a well in the centre of the flour/yeast/herb mixture and add the liquid gradually, working the mixture in with a wooden or silicone spoon, or your hands.

Lightly flour your work surface and tip the dough on to it. Knead and stretch the dough for about 10 minutes. Lightly oil the inside of the bowl, put the dough back into it, cover with a clean tea towel and leave to rise until doubled in size. This takes about half an hour, but the time varies depending on the temperature of the room.

When the dough is risen, knock the air out of it by tipping it back on to a lightly floured work surface. Gently shape into a round and pop into a lightly oiled or silicone 1lb loaf tin (approximately 17 x 7 x 6cm). Cover with cling film or a clean plastic bag over the top like a tent and leave for 30 minutes to prove. A little before the end of the proving time, put on the oven to 220°C/425°F/gas 7 to preheat.

Score the top of the loaf with a sharp knife and pop it into the preheated oven for 30 minutes.

The loaf should sound hollow on the bottom when tapped. Remove from the oven, tip out of the tin and allow to cool on a wire rack. Then slice the loaf and eat!

PENNY PIZZAS

I make penny pizzas as a way of using up leftovers such as Mumma Jack's Best Ever Chilli (see page 70) or Lentil Bolognese (see page 64) – but they are just as good topped with a dollop of tomato purée and some grated cheese. Or they are a good way to use up sliced mushy tomatoes that have passed their best and the dry ends of cheese. I have collected novelty cookie cutters over the years, so Small Boy often asks for 'duckie pizza' or 'lorry pizza' – resulting in a frantic delve through my kitchen to find the right one.

Makes 14 mini-pizzas
(using an 8cm cookie cutter)

250g plain flour, plus extra
to knead the dough

a 7g sachet of fast-acting
dried yeast

optional: a pinch of salt

1 tablespoon oil, plus extra to
oil the baking tray

200ml lukewarm water

3 tablespoons tomato purée

optional: a sprinkle of dried
mixed herbs

Topping ideas: mozzarella cheese, any grated cheese, chopped onion, ham and pineapple, ham and sweetcorn, leftover Bolognese sauce or leftover chilli . . . The possibilities are endless!

Measure the flour and yeast into a large mixing bowl and add the salt, if using. Make a well in the centre of the flour, add the oil and most of the water, and stir together with a spoon to make a soft, sticky dough. Add more water if required.

Tip the dough on to a floured work surface, lightly knead for a few minutes and shape into a round. Pop it back into the mixing bowl, cover with cling film or a clean tea towel and leave for an hour to rise, or until doubled in size.

When the dough has risen, tip out on to the floured work surface and roll out with a rolling pin. I make mine less than 0.5cm thick but it's up to you. Bear in mind when rolling out the dough that the bases will double in thickness when cooked. Cut out dough circles or shapes using your choice of cutter, transferring these mini pizza bases on to a lightly oiled baking tray as you go. (You may need to do them in batches!)

Preheat the oven to 180°C/350°F/gas 4. Top each dough pizza base with a thin spread of tomato purée, the dried herbs, if using, and your topping of choice. Pop the baking tray into the oven for 10 minutes, until the mini pizzas are slightly crisp around the edges. Larger pizzas may need a longer cooking time.

TIPS: The penny pizzas will keep in the fridge, covered, for 2 to 3 days, making them ideal for little lunches.

Allow to cool completely and freeze any leftovers. They will keep for 3 months in the freezer, and can be reheated in a low oven.

To make a large pizza traybake, roll out the dough into a rectangle the size of your baking tray instead of cutting into individual mini pizzas. You'll need to bake this a little longer until crisp.

For quicker pizzas, halve a pitta bread, spread with tomato purée and top with a topping of your choice. Cook for 10 minutes at 180°C/350°F/gas 4 for a speedy snack.

WHITE CHOCOLATE TEA BREAD

This came about because I LOVE chocolate-chip brioche – so I decided to try to make some chocolate-chip bread as a replacement. Unfortunately, though, the chocolate chips all melted into the dough as I added warm water and I ended up with this Chocolate Tea Bread instead – but it was still delicious! Then I experimented with tea and white chocolate and stumbled on something heavenly. Bliss!

Makes 1 small loaf

275g self-raising flour (or 275g plain flour and 2 teaspoons baking powder or bicarbonate of soda), plus extra to knead the dough

a 7g sachet of fast-acting dried yeast

50g sugar

200g white chocolate

25g butter, plus extra to grease the loaf tin

150ml boiling water with a tea bag steeped in it, left to cool slightly (trust me on this one!)

TIP: To make a proper buttery-type chocolate brioche bread, fold in the chocolate chunks when kneading the dough instead of earlier on.

Measure the flour, yeast and sugar into a large mixing bowl.

Break the chocolate into chunks. It's up to you how you do this; I put mine into a freezer bag and bash it with the flat end of a rolling pin, or you could use a wood mallet in a similar set-up, or chop the chocolate on a work surface with a big sharp knife if you're cheffy and adept at that sort of thing. Tip the chocolate chunks into the bowl with the flour, yeast and sugar.

Add the butter to the bowl and pour in the warm black tea, then stir together with a wooden spoon until well combined and the mixture has turned into a pliable, soft, sticky dough.

Tip out the dough on to a generously floured work surface and knead for a good 10 minutes. I always notice when I've got oil or butter in a bread dough because it has a beautiful silken texture and eminent pliability. If you've made bread before, you'll notice the difference. When kneaded, pat the dough into a rugby ball shape, cover and leave on the side for 20 minutes to rise.

Once the dough has risen, transfer it into a lightly greased 1 lb loaf tin (approximately 17 x 7 x 6cm) to prove. Cover with oiled cling film or a tea towel and leave in a warm place for a further half an hour. A little before the end of the proving time, put on the oven to 180°C/350°F/gas 4 to preheat.

When the dough has risen again, put the tin into the preheated oven for 40 minutes to bake, and wait for the smell of chocolate and bread to permeate your house. If the top of the loaf starts to brown before it's done, remove from the oven, cover the tin with tin foil and pop it back in for the remainder of the baking time.

Remove the tin from the oven, allow the loaf to cool on a wire rack and turn out ready to slice and eat.

SUPER SOUPS

I first started making my own soup from one of the 'stew packs' of root vegetables you can buy in the supermarket, along with a stock cube and a handful of herbs. I now add beans, lentils and pulses to a lot of my soups, packing in protein and making them more filling – ideal for a late-night dinner or a lunch that will see you through the afternoon. Leftovers of any of these soup recipes can be frozen in an ice cube tray or small airtight container, to make an instant pasta sauce. If you are a soup-making novice, start with the Really Tomatoey Basilly Soup (see page 44) – and don't be afraid to experiment once you've got the hang of it!

If you buy only one item of fancy kitchen equipment, you'd be best off buying a blender because it's so brilliant for soups. Mine is from a supermarket value range, cost under a tenner and has lasted me three years so far! Hand blenders are even cheaper.

LOVE SOUP

There are many different recipes entitled Love Soup – I've seen some rich chicken soup recipes, some with heady garlic and some deep red tomato soup ones. By chance, the ingredients for this were what I had kicking around in the fridge last Valentine's Day, so this warming carrot, ginger and onion soup is mine. Nothing says 'I love you' quite like sweet roasted vegetables, blended into a home-made silky soft soup. Not in my book, anyway.

Serves 2 (of course!)

3 tablespoons vegetable oil

zest and juice of ½ a lemon or
1 tablespoon bottled lemon juice

1 clove of garlic

1 small piece of fresh ginger
(approximately 1cm) or
1 teaspoon ground ginger

a fistful of fresh coriander

a fistful of fresh parsley,
plus extra to garnish

1 onion

2 large carrots

1 potato

1 vegetable stock cube

Preheat the oven to 180°C/350°F/gas 4.

First make the marinade for the vegetables. Measure the oil into a tea cup, jug or other small receptacle. Finely grate the lemon zest into the oil. Peel and crush the garlic, and peel and grate the ginger, then add them too. Finely chop the herbs into the mixture. Squeeze the lemon juice in – as much of it as you can squish out – then stir together and set aside.

Peel the onion, chop into quarters and place in a roasting dish. Wash then chop the carrots into thick rounds and add to the roasting dish. Peel and dice the potato and put it in too. Pour the marinade over the top and shake to coat the vegetables. Pop the roasting dish into the preheated oven for an hour or so, shaking occasionally to loosen the vegetables and re-coat them in the marinade.

When the carrots and potatoes are tender, remove the vegetables from the oven and tip into a food processor. Dissolve the stock cube in 500ml of boiling water and pour this stock into the food processor (to cover the vegetables). Blend until smooth, and serve with a flourish of parsley and a smile.

TIPS: Add a swirl of natural yoghurt and/or honey at the end, to make this soup extra special.

Since it's quite a lot of effort for a soup, make double the amount and freeze half of it to have an indulgent treat on tap.

You can replace the fresh carrots with a small tin of carrots. Simply drain and rinse them, and add in place of the chopped carrots – halving the roasting time, since they will cook more quickly than their fresh counterparts. The same rule applies to tinned potatoes, but as these tend to be small, use four or five.

REALLY TOMATOEY BASILLY SOUP

This is so simple that I feel cheeky calling it a recipe, but it's one for all those folks that say to me, 'Oh, I'd love to make soup but I don't know where to start.' Well, start here and see where it takes you. There's even some chopping of vegetables involved, so brace yourselves. Tinned soup contains among other things modified maize starch, whey powder, ascorbic acid and other things that I'm not entirely sure what they are – so make my own and get something good inside you.

Serves 2

1 onion

1 large carrot

1 potato

1 vegetable stock cube, dissolved in 400ml boiling water

1 x 400g carton or tin of chopped tomatoes

a generous handful of fresh basil or 2 teaspoons dried basil

Peel and slice the onion, and wash and chop the carrot and potato into small pieces. (I make mine 0.5cm thick or less so they cook faster and blend more easily. I also leave the skins on for all the extra goodness.)

Put all the vegetables into a saucepan and pour in the stock to cover. Tip the chopped tomatoes over the top, add the basil and bring to an enthusiastic boil.

Reduce the heat to a simmer and leave to its own souper-duper devices for approximately 20 minutes, until the vegetables are tender. Test by poking a fork into one of them – if it goes through easily, then they're done.

Blend in a food processor until smooth, and serve hot.

TIP: This will keep in the fridge for about 3 days – but use your discretion. I keep my fridge extra cold so food lasts longer. Cool and freeze in an airtight container for approximately 3 months.

TOMATO AND HARICOT BEAN SOUP

This simple staple started off as a tin of baked beans, thoroughly rinsed, plus a carton of chopped tomatoes – out of which I made a hearty, filling soup suitable for lunch or a light dinner. Baked beans are normally just haricot or borlotti beans slathered in that bright orange tomato sauce.

Serves 4

1 medium onion

2 cloves of garlic

1 carrot

500ml beef or vegetable stock

1 x 400g tin of cannelloni, haricot or butter beans

a handful of fresh thyme or rosemary

1 x 400g carton or tin of chopped tomatoes

Peel and chop the onion, peel and finely chop the garlic, wash and chop the carrot. Put them all into a saucepan and cover with the stock.

Drain and rinse the tinned beans, then throw them into the pan. Add the herbs and the chopped tomatoes, then simmer for 30 minutes until the veg are soft.

This soup can be served chunky – by tipping half into a blender, pulsing and mixing the purée back in with the chunky half in the pan – or smooth, by pulsing the lot in a blender.

TIPS: For a lighter summer version, add a splash of lemon juice, use chicken stock in place of the beef and parsley instead of the woody herbs.

Use less stock for a thicker mixture, which once blended can be frozen in ice cube moulds and used as a delicious pasta sauce.

CARROT AND CORIANDER SOUP

Carrot and coriander soup is a classic fresh soup that crops up everywhere – from cardboard cartons in the supermarket to smart restaurant menus. Here's my simple recipe for making your own. I often substitute the fresh potato and carrot for their tinned sisters, for an even easier version.

Serves 2

1 onion

4 carrots

1 potato

1 vegetable stock cube

a fistful of fresh coriander, chopped

a fistful of fresh parsley, chopped

Peel and chop the onion and place in a medium-sized saucepan. Wash and chop the carrots and potato (without peeling), and add to the pan. Pour in cold water to cover (approximately 500ml), crumble in the stock cube and bring to the boil.

Add the parsley and coriander. Reduce the heat to low and simmer for 20 minutes, until the carrots and potatoes are tender and yield easily when prodded with a fork.

Remove from the heat and blend in a food processor until smooth. Serve hot.

TIPS: Add a scant ½ teaspoon of ground cumin or turmeric for a spicy soup.

Use less water (only 300ml) to make a lovely carroty pasta sauce instead of a soup.

CARROT, CUMIN AND KIDNEY BEAN SOUP

This recipe came about after seeing the tins of soup in the supermarket and thinking, 'I can do better than that.' So rather than stocking up on thin tomato soup with suspiciously few tomatoes, I thought I'd treat myself to some cheap, versatile, protein-packed spicy goodness instead. The quantities here make four generous portions.

Serves 4

1 onion

2 tablespoons oil

1 heaped tablespoon ground cumin

300g carrots

1 vegetable or chicken stock cube, dissolved in 500ml boiling water

1 x 400g tin of red kidney beans

Peel and chop the onion and put into a medium-sized saucepan with the oil and cumin. Wash and chop the carrots and add to the pan. Cook on a low heat for a few minutes until the onion is starting to turn golden.

Pour the stock into the pan and bring to the boil. Turn down and simmer for 20 minutes or until the carrots are tender.

Drain and rinse the kidney beans well, add to the pan and heat through. Tip everything into a blender and pulse until smooth.

TIPS: Add a few tablespoons of natural yoghurt after blending for a creamy taste.

You can add a handful of cooked red lentils to the leftover blended soup to turn it into a thick, spicy pasta sauce. Alternatively, to make a thicker soup, add rinsed lentils along with the chopped carrots and cook in the stock.

Pretty much the same ingredients are used for the Carrot, Cumin and Kidney Bean Burgers (see page 63), so why not buy in bulk and make them both in the same week – or even at the same time!

FEISTY SOUP

I make this for myself whenever I feel as though I am coming down with a cold. You know – when you've got that shaky, exhausted feeling and air of general self-pity. Instead of spending a fortune on various over-the-counter paracetamol and lemon drinks, I drag myself into the kitchen and cook myself a cure. This is called feisty soup for a reason: it's a bit like hot and sour Chinese soup in a way, and if this doesn't help shift whatever is wrong with you, I'm not sure what will. I've combined lots of natural goodies that have antioxidant and other nutritional qualities – garlic for goodness, chillies to fire up your system, tomatoes for vitamin C and lemon and ginger to cleanse and revitalize. I'm no expert, but this works for me every time.

Serves 2

1 onion

1 fat clove of garlic

a thick slice of fresh ginger

1 red chilli

a splash of oil

1 x 400g carton or tin of chopped tomatoes

1 vegetable stock cube, dissolved in 200ml boiling water

juice of ½ a lemon or 2 teaspoons bottled lemon juice

a handful of parsley

Peel and chop the onion, garlic and ginger, chop the chilli, and put them all into a medium-sized saucepan with the oil. Cook on a low heat until the onion is softened. Tip in the chopped tomatoes, pour in the stock and add the lemon juice. Chop the parsley and add to the saucepan as well.

Simmer away for about 20 minutes, until the onion and ginger have softened.

Blitz in a blender to achieve your desired consistency. I leave mine a bit chunky but it can be blended smooth.

Eat, and feel better soon!

TIPS: If making this soup for little mouths, do not chop the chilli or use the seeds inside. Instead, halve the chilli down the middle and rinse it under a cold tap to remove the seeds, then add to the soup whole during cooking. Remove before blending.

Any remaining soup will keep in an airtight container in the fridge for 2 days, or in the freezer for 3 months.

The soup can be left whole and chunky as a fiery sauce to form part of a more substantial meal. Omit the stock, stir through a few handfuls of cooked prawns and some green beans, and serve with spaghetti or noodles, as in the photo.

ROASTED COURGETTE AND MINT SOUP

Plain courgette soup sounds like a sad affair – but roasting these abundant green vegetables brings out a delicious sweetness, perfect for a bowl of warm, comforting soup accompanied by crusty bread. Make it thicker for a delicious pasta sauce that can be frozen in ice cube trays for convenience. Add a tablespoon of natural yoghurt and some Greek cheese like feta or goat's cheese for a particularly luxurious, creamy version of the soup.

Serves 4 as a light lunch,
2 as a main meal

500g courgettes

1 onion

1 clove of garlic

1 tablespoon oil

500ml vegetable stock

a handful of fresh mint

hard strong cheese, to serve

Preheat the oven to 180°C/350°F/gas 4.

Cut the ends off the courgettes and roughly dice, peel the onion and roughly chop, peel and finely slice the garlic. Brush the oil around a roasting dish and scatter in all the vegetables. Roast in the preheated oven for 20 minutes, or until the courgettes are golden and just starting to crisp around the edges. The roasted veg into a blender along with the stock and the mint, and pulse until smooth. Pour the soup into a saucepan on a medium heat and warm through.

Serve in bowls with a grating of cheese over the top.

Tip the roasted veg into a blender along with the stock and the mint, and pulse until smooth. Pour the soup into a saucepan on a medium heat and warm through.

Serve in bowls with a grating of cheese over the top.

RED WINE AND MUSHROOM SOUP

Mushrooms are one of my staple ingredients, being both cheaply available at supermarkets and greengrocers, and simple enough to grow at home. I'm a tactile cook, so I like to break them up with my hands instead of slicing them, but it doesn't make a difference to the end result of the recipe. If you like this and you have red wine and mushrooms left over, try making the Earthy Red Wine and Mushroom Risotto (see page 107).

Serves 2

200g mushrooms

1 onion

1 clove of garlic

1 vegetable stock cube, dissolved in 300ml boiling water

50ml red wine

a handful of chopped thyme, plus extra to garnish

Gently clean any excess earth from the mushrooms with a clean tea towel, and break or slice them up. Peel and chop the onion and peel and crush the garlic. Put the mushrooms into a saucepan along with the stock, wine, thyme, onion and garlic.

Bring to the boil, then reduce down to a simmer for 20 minutes for all the flavours to meld. Remove from the heat and pulse in a blender.

Serve with extra chopped thyme to garnish.

TIPS: Replace the red wine with white wine and add a tablespoon of natural yoghurt just before blending for a lighter, more traditional creamy mushroom soup. Garnish with some grated strong hard cheese.

Mix any leftover soup with a carton or tin of chopped tomatoes and some cooked red or brown lentils for a hearty pasta sauce that can be frozen in portions, and defrosted for a quick and easy dinner.

MEXICAN CHOCOLATE, CHILLI AND BLACK BEAN SOUP

I knocked up this soup when I had a piteous cold last winter (yes, another one!). It combines onions and garlic for detoxifying goodness with chillies to fire you up, tomatoes and carrots for essential vitamin C, beans for protein and chocolate because it's a solution to almost everything. Plus dark chocolate and red wine are good for you, don't you know? But putting all the science to one side, this is delicious, filling and surprising – so even if you don't have a cold, make this soup!

Serves 2

100g dried black beans

1 onion

1 clove of garlic

1 small red chilli or a pinch of chilli flakes

a generous shake of paprika

a generous shake of ground cumin

a splash of oil

1 carrot

30ml red wine

1 x 400g carton or tin of chopped tomatoes

1 vegetable stock cube

3 squares dark chocolate (approximately 20g)

fresh parsley, to garnish

Put your beans in to soak the night before, or early in the morning if you're going to be cooking that evening. Place them in a bowl, cover with fresh cold water and then some, and cover the bowl with cling film. Leave for a minimum of 8 hours to soak.

When soaked, drain and thoroughly rinse your beans. Put them into a saucepan with fresh water and bring to the boil for approximately 10 minutes, then turn down to a simmer.

Meanwhile, peel and slice the onion and garlic, and chop the chilli (reserving a couple of slices for a garnish), then put them all into a saucepan along with the paprika and cumin. Add the oil and cook over a low heat until the onions and garlic soften.

Wash and chop the carrot, and add to the saucepan. Pour the red wine and tomatoes in, and stir through. Crumble in the stock cube, then add the dark chocolate and 400ml boiling water. Drain the beans and tip into the pan. Stir and leave to simmer for 20 minutes, or until the carrot is tender.

If you like, pulse the soup in a blender until smooth. (I prefer to leave mine just slightly chunky, but if pulsed thoroughly, this makes a deliciously silky texture.) Serve hot, garnished with a sprig of fresh parsley and a slice of red chilli in each bowl.

TIPS: Grill pitta breads with cheese inside – until it melts – and serve these dunked in the soup for a seriously tasty treat!

Swirl cream, natural yoghurt or crème fraîche on top before serving.

This recipe uses almost identical ingredients to Mumma Jack's Best Ever Chilli (see page 70), so why not make them together?

SIMPLE SPICED POTATO SOUP

This is one of my go-to recipes, a whatever-happens-to-be-in-the-cupboard special. I sometimes add a chopped chilli to the onion, and some coriander from my window ledge herb box, but I have given the basic recipe below – feel free to customize it as you wish. When it comes to my lunch, I can be an impatient oik so I tend to chop the tinned potatoes into small cubes. It makes no difference to the final product, just means that they cook quicker. I like to serve this soup with pitta bread.

Serves 2

1 onion

a splash of oil

a few generous pinches of ground cumin or turmeric (whichever you have available)

1 x 500g tin of potatoes (approximate drained weight)

1 chicken stock cube, dissolved in 200ml boiling water

150ml natural yoghurt

Peel and chop the onion and put into a saucepan with the oil and cumin. Cook on a low heat for around 10 minutes to soften the onions into a spicy sweetness.

Drain the tinned potatoes, cut into small cubes and tip into the saucepan. Pour in the stock and simmer for 10 minutes, or until the potatoes are very soft.

Tip everything into a blender along with the yoghurt and blitz until smooth and creamy. Add more water if necessary – I find different tins of potatoes come up differently.

Serve and enjoy!

TIPS: I sometimes like to add spinach to this soup and a tiny dab of mustard, to make it a bit more exciting.

If there are any Spiced Spinach Potatoes left over (see Saag Aloo recipe on page 137), this is a brilliant use for them. Just add in place of the tinned potatoes.

ONION SOUP WITH RED WINE

This is a twist on the classic onion soup recipe, a warming wintry version with red wine. You can blend it smooth or leave it as a broth with chunks of onion.

Serves 4

2 cloves of garlic

500g red or white onions

1 tablespoon oil

2 sprigs of fresh thyme

50ml red wine

500ml beef or vegetable stock

optional: 1 teaspoon Marmite (if using vegetable stock)

Peel and thinly slice the garlic and onions and dice the potato and put into a medium non-stick saucepan with the oil and thyme leaves. Put the pan on a low heat and cook for about 10 minutes, until the onions are soft. Take care not to let them brown, and stir occasionally to stop them from sticking to the pan.

Pour in the wine and simmer for a few minutes before adding the stock, and Marmite, if using. Turn the heat up to bring to the boil.

Reduce to a simmer and cook for 20 minutes, then serve.

TIPS: For a lighter summery version, replace the red wine with white wine and stir through a dollop of natural yoghurt just before serving.

To make this go further, add a handful of red or brown lentils.

AVGOLEMONO

Avgolemono is the soup of my childhood – my first memory is of being at my Aunty Helen's house in Plymouth in the summer holidays, tucking into bowls of this soup after the long drive there. My father made Avgolemono Soup at home, as did my mother, and we often had a pot of it sitting on the back of the stove. For years I asked for the recipe and they would always smile and tell me that it was a secret. They will read this and shake their heads, as this is probably not their recipe, but it is taken from a book given to me by my grandmother – *The Cypriots at Table* – and has served me well over the past few years. My parents' Avgolemono always came with scraps of chicken floating in it, whereas Aunty Helen's did not. Some Greek restaurants add parsley to it, but I believe that is more for prettiness than taste. Simple, honest food is sometimes the best of all. These quantities make enough for 2 people with seconds!

Serves 2

600ml vegetable or chicken stock

100g rice

2 eggs

zest and juice of 1 lemon or 2 tablespoons bottled lemon juice, plus extra to serve

Bring the stock to the boil in a medium-sized saucepan, then add the rice and reduce to a simmer for 15 minutes.

Break the eggs into a small bowl, grate in the lemon zest, squeeze in the juice and beat well. Add a few tablespoons of the hot stock to the egg mixture, beating it in quickly and thoroughly. Repeat. This step is very important – if you simply tip the egg mixture into the stock, you will end up with a pan of chicken stock with some scrambled eggs floating on the top. I learned this the hard way!

Once you have beaten in stock to the eggs two or three times, pour the egg mixture into the saucepan with the rice, and stir well to combine.

Serve the soup with extra lemon juice squeezed over the top, to taste.

TIP: If you have a roast chicken carcass, this is an ideal place to use up all those 'bits' of chicken. Add the carcass to the pan with the stock and remove it before you add the eggs, picking all the shreds of chicken off with your hands and adding them back to the soup.

SPICED LENTIL SOUP

This spiced lentil soup is comforting winter food – I keep tinned carrots, tomatoes and a bag of lentils on standby for those evenings when Small Boy is already tucked up in bed and snoozing and there's not much else in the fridge or kitchen cupboard. I've used red lentils here, but brown lentils or green ones are just as delicious. Take this recipe as a guide to start experimenting with.

Serves 4

1 onion

2 cloves of garlic

1 small red chilli or a pinch of the dried stuff

2 carrots or 300g tinned carrots (drained weight)

1 tablespoon oil

1 teaspoon ground cumin or cumin seeds

a handful of fresh coriander or parsley

1 x 400g carton or tin of chopped tomatoes

200g dried red lentils, rinsed

Peel and slice the onion, peel and finely chop the garlic, finely slice the chilli and wash and slice the carrots. Put the oil into a medium heavy-based saucepan, add the vegetables plus the chilli and cumin, and cook on a low heat, stirring to soften. Chop the coriander or parsley and add to the pan.

When the onions have started to soften, pour over the chopped tomatoes and add the lentils. Add 1 litre of water (that's 4 cups of water for every cup of lentils). Stir and turn the heat up to bring to the boil, then reduce to a simmer. Simmer for 20 minutes or until the lentils have swollen.

Serve chunky or pulse in a blender until smooth.

TIPS: Thicken leftover soup with extra cooked lentils to make a pasta sauce, or simply use less water in the first place. Toss with pasta and grate some cheese on top for added deliciousness.

For a richer-flavoured soup, add a glass of red or white wine and reduce the amount of water slightly.

MUSHY PEA SOUP

I've detested peas since I was a child, scraping them from the sides of any violated chips in disgust whenever my parents treated us to a 'chippy dinner'. However, somehow a tin of mushy peas always invariably ends up in my store cupboard and I was determined to make something from it that even I would eat. An egg and a blob of yoghurt later, and I'm really rather happy with this. Omit the stock for a bright green pasta sauce that little ones will either be delighted by or deeply suspicious of!

Serves 4

1 egg

1 x 300g tin of mushy peas

zest and juice of ½ a lemon or 1 tablespoon bottled lemon juice

200ml vegetable or chicken stock

100ml natural yoghurt

optional: black pepper, to serve

First, soft boil or poach your egg for just shy of the 4 minutes recommended cooking time once immersed in boiling water.

Remove the egg from the pan and peel (if soft boiled), then pop into a blender with the mushy peas, lemon zest and juice, stock and yoghurt. Pulse to blend, then tip the soup back into a saucepan to warm through.

Serve hot with black pepper sprinkled or ground on top, if you have any.

TIPS: Include 1 chopped onion sautéed in a splash of oil and an extra egg for a gourmet version.

Add a fistful of mint to the ingredients for blending to create a refreshing pea and mint soup.

For amazing mushy pea pasta, make this soup thicker by using less stock (or less water to make up the stock), then toss the resulting pea sauce with cooked pasta and top with a handful of grated cheese.

Add some pieces of crisped ham or bacon as a topping for a sort of pea and ham soup.

BEANS, PULSES AND LENTILS

Before I found myself on a very limited budget, I hadn't really cooked with beans as a food in their own right. I'd popped a tin of kidney beans in a chilli, or some white beans in a casserole, but I was a bit perplexed by them. However, beans and pulses are so much cheaper than meat that I began to work them into my meals. I replaced the meat in my chilli recipe (see page 70) with two kinds of beans, added them to soups, and hunted through my old Cypriot cook books for a recipe for Gigantes Plaki (see page 73) – and now I wouldn't be without beans in the kitchen. They also make a great substitute for minced meat. If boiled until soft and mashed, they can be shaped into burgers or falafels – experiment and enjoy!

You can use dried beans and pulses in place of tinned ones, but as a rule you need to soak them overnight, drain, thoroughly rinse and rapidly boil for 10 minutes to remove any toxins. Then simmer on a medium heat for up to 2 hours, or until softened. I usually use tinned chickpeas, though, unless I'm making a slow-cooked stew or curry. They are more expensive than buying a bag of dried ones, but dried chickpeas take much longer than other beans and pulses to cook on the hob, up to two hours, even after soaking overnight.

CARROT, CUMIN AND KIDNEY BEAN BURGERS

This burger is where the media storm began and, dubbed 'the 9p burger' because of the low cost of the ingredients used to make it, it's one of my most popular recipes. A can of value range red kidney beans is a cheap but excellent source of protein and I built a lot of my early cooking around it. When my toddler asked me for burgers for tea, I made him these, and they became a firm staple in my household. I triple the recipe to make a batch of them and freeze them in patties to whip out at a moment's notice and fry on a low heat. I serve mine in a pitta bread, roll or sliced white muffin, with rice and green vegetables.

Makes 4 burgers

1 x 400g tin of kidney beans

1 onion, peeled and finely chopped

1 carrot, grated

1 teaspoon ground cumin

a handful of fresh coriander, finely chopped

a splash of oil, plus 2 tablespoons to fry the burgers

1 heaped teaspoon flour, plus extra to shape the burgers

Drain the kidney beans and rinse in cold water to wash away the 'tinned' taste. Put into a saucepan and cover with cold water. Bring to the boil, then simmer for 10 minutes to soften.

Put the onion, carrot, cumin and coriander into a medium sauté pan. Add the splash of oil and cook on a low heat to soften. When the kidney beans have softened, drain and add to the carrots and onions. Take off the heat and mash together until you have a smoothish purée (like mashed potato consistency). Stir in the flour.

Heat the 2 tablespoons of oil in a frying pan on a medium heat. With floured hands, take a quarter of the burger mixture and roll it into a ball, about the size of a golf ball. Make three more balls with the remaining mixture. Place one in the oil and flatten gently with a fork to make the burger shape. Depending on the size of your pan, you may be able to cook all the burgers at once or need to do them in batches – unless you're freezing some of the uncooked patties. Cook for a few minutes on one side, before turning. The burgers need to be handled with care as they can be quite fragile! When cooked on both sides, remove from the pan and serve – eating them hot.

TIPS: Make the burger mixture in advance and pop into the fridge for a few hours – it firms up nicely and is less fragile while cooking. It will keep for 2 days if covered so can be made well in advance.

This recipe uses very similar ingredients to the Carrot, Cumin and Kidney Bean Soup (see page 47), so why not make both at the same time.

Instead of making burgers, shape into golf balls and shallow fry for 10 minutes to make 'meatballs'. When cooked, tip a carton of chopped tomatoes over the top and stir through to coat and heat, and serve with rice or pasta. The balls are also good cold in a pitta bread with mango chutney for next day's lunch. Like the burgers, they can be made in a batch and frozen before cooking.

LENTIL BOLOGNESE

This meat-free Bolognese sauce is perfect over a bowl of pasta and topped with a handful of grated cheese. Allow 70 to 100g of dried pasta per person. I like to eat mine with some garlic bread as well, to mop up any leftover sauce.

Serves 2

1 onion

1 clove of garlic

1 carrot

1 tablespoon oil

a fistful of fresh thyme

a fistful of fresh parsley

1 vegetable stock cube

50ml red wine

1 x 400g carton or tin of chopped tomatoes

100g dried brown lentils, rinsed

optional: 2 tablespoons tomato purée or tomato ketchup, to thicken the sauce

grated hard strong cheese, to serve

Peel and slice the onion, peel and crush the garlic, and put both into a large sauté or non-stick frying pan. Wash the carrot, then grate into the pan and add the oil. Put on a low heat and fry gently, stirring occasionally to prevent sticking and burning.

Chop the herbs – I place mine in a tea cup and cut into them with kitchen scissors – then add to the carrot, onion and garlic in the pan.

When the onions are softened, crumble in the stock cube and add the wine, chopped tomatoes, tomato purée or ketchup, if using, and lentils. Stir in and simmer over a low heat for 20 minutes, or until the lentils are al dente (I like them to have a bit of a bite). You may need to add a small tea cup of water if the sauce looks too dry, but use your judgement.

Once the lentils are done, it's ready to serve. As with any Bolognese, this is delicious topped with a grating of cheese.

TIPS: You can use up any spare Bolognese mixture as a topping for Penny Pizzas (see page 36).

This is also good cold or reheated, stuffed in a pitta or wrap with some grated cheese for next day's lunch.

WARM CHICKPEA SALAD WITH BACON AND OLIVES

This speedy lunch was born of the bottom of a jar of sliced black olives, some scraps of bacon and a tin of chickpeas lurking in the cupboard. A small jar of sliced black olives goes a long way – use them in pasta dishes or as a savoury spread on toast, perhaps.

Serves 2

1 x 400g tin of chickpeas

1 onion

2 cloves of garlic

3 tablespoons oil

1 tablespoon lemon juice

2 heaped tablespoons finely chopped black olives

200g bacon

a handful of fresh parsley, finely chopped

salad leaves, to serve

Drain and thoroughly rinse the chickpeas, and pop them into a saucepan of cold water on a high heat. Bring to the boil, reduce to a simmer and cook through for about 10 minutes to soften.

Meanwhile, peel and finely chop the onion and garlic. Put into a small frying pan or non-stick saucepan with the oil, lemon juice and olives. Chop the bacon into small pieces – the size of pancetta cubes – and add to the pan. Cook together on a medium heat to crisp the bacon and soften the onion and olives. Toss the parsley into the pan.

When the chickpeas are softened, drain and tip back into the saucepan. Add the bacon, olives, onion and any oil from the pan, and stir well to combine.

Serve hot or cold, tossed with salad leaves.

TIP: This will keep for a day or two in the fridge and makes an excellent packed lunch dish – either as a chickpea salad or mashed lightly and spooned into pitta breads.

MIXED BEAN GOULASH

I never tire of this quick, simple meal. Originally adapted from a beef goulash recipe, but tweaked and tampered with in the way that all recipes are, it has become a sweet and spicy staple in my household and doesn't disappoint. I use cheap baked beans in place of haricot beans, as they are simply haricot or borlotti beans slathered in sauce – but usually for a third of the price of a tin of plain haricot or borlotti beans! Eat warm on toast, with rice or stuffed in a pitta bread with lashings of cheese for lunch. Eat from a bowl, water it down and eat as a soup, or eat it straight from the pan in the name of 'testing'. Or, for a slightly Mexican twist, have it with tortillas, some grated cheese, sliced red onion and iceberg lettuce, with lime to squeeze over.

Serves 4–6

1 x 400g tin of red kidney beans

1 x 400g tin of baked beans

1 onion

1 fat clove of garlic or a generous shake of the dried stuff

4 tablespoons oil

3 teaspoons paprika

1 x 400g carton or tin of chopped tomatoes

1 teaspoon Marmite or Vegemite

1 vegetable stock cube

1 teaspoon sugar

First, drain and rinse the beans. Empty the kidney beans and the baked beans into a colander, and blast under cold water to get rid of the tinned taste, and the cheap sauce from the baked beans. When well rinsed, set to one side.

Peel and chop the onion, and peel and finely slice the garlic. Place in a sauté or large non-stick frying pan with the oil and paprika, and fry on a low heat until the onion is softened. Add the chopped tomatoes, Marmite or Vegemite, crumbled stock cube, sugar and half a tin of water, and stir well. Simmer gently for 15 minutes until thickened and glossy.

Tip in the colander of rinsed beans, stir to mix well and heat through for 10 minutes. Serve, devour, have seconds and enjoy!

TIPS: To make it cheaper, leave out the Marmite and use a beef stock cube instead of the vegetable one.

Blitz half in a blender with a little extra water until smooth, then stir in the reserved half to make a chunky, spicy soup.

This stew also freezes beautifully, if allowed to cool and stored in an airtight container, or keeps in the fridge for 2 to 3 days.

CHICKPEA, CARROT AND CORIANDER FALAFELS

This recipe uses tinned chickpeas, as dried chickpeas take a long time to cook. They need to be soaked overnight, boiled for 10 minutes, then simmered for around 2 hours, so I buy them tinned for speedy results. If you want to use dried chickpeas, use half the quantity of tinned, i.e. 200g in this recipe. I like to serve the falafels accompanied by couscous made up with vegetable or chicken stock, lemon juice and coriander, and with green beans or another green vegetable.

Makes 12-ish falafels
(4–6 per person)

1 onion

1 carrot

a generous shake of ground cumin

1 tablespoon oil, plus 2 tablespoons to fry the falafels

1 x 400g tin of chickpeas, drained and rinsed thoroughly

a handful of chopped parsley

a handful of chopped coriander

1 tablespoon flour, plus extra to shape the falafels

Peel and finely chop the onion and wash and grate the carrot. (I grate the onion too so it's finer, but it's a pain to do!) Put into a frying pan, add the cumin and fry together in the 1 tablespoon of oil over a low heat for a few minutes until softened.

Tip the cooked onion and carrot into a large mixing bowl along with the chickpeas, add the chopped parsley and coriander and stir in the flour. Mash it all together with a potato masher or fork until the chickpeas have broken down into a mush. The oil from the carrots and onion will help combine the chickpeas together, but you may need to add up to 2 tablespoons of water so the mixture can be shaped.

Flour your hands and mould the mixture into about 12 golf ball shapes. Heat the remaining 2 tablespoons of oil in the sauté pan and fry the balls until golden brown and slightly crispy on the outside – this will take about 10 minutes.

TIP: Instead of making falafels, shape the mixture into 4 burger patties and fry on each side. These are delicious with mango chutney or ketchup.

MUMMA JACK'S BEST-EVER CHILLI

This chilli is adapted from a beef chilli recipe by Gordon Ramsay. I simply left out the beef and halved the wine to make it cheaper – plus, of course, Mr Ramsay doesn't use a tin of cheap baked beans in his version! I've tweaked and fiddled with it so much over the years that now it's not Gordon's chilli, it's Mumma Jack's.

Serves 4

1 x 400g tin of red kidney beans

1 x 400g tin of baked beans in tomato sauce

1 onion

1 small chilli, chopped

a shake of paprika

a shake of ground cumin

a splash of oil

75ml red table wine

1 x 400g carton or tin of chopped tomatoes

1 vegetable stock cube

3 squares dark chocolate

Tip both tins of beans into a colander and rinse thoroughly. If you are using baked beans in tomato sauce, make sure to rinse it all off. Pop the beans into a saucepan, cover with water and bring to the boil. Boil rapidly for 10 minutes, then reduce to a gentle simmer.

Peel and dice the onion and put into a large sauté pan along with the chopped chilli, paprika and cumin. Add the oil and cook on a low heat until the onion softens into a spicy sweetness. Pour in the wine, add the chopped tomatoes and crumble in the stock cube, then simmer all together on a low heat.

When the beans have softened, drain and tip into the sauce. Add the chocolate and stir until the beans are mixed through and the chocolate is melted.

TIPS: This chilli will keep in the fridge for up to 3 days if allowed to cool and stored in an airtight container.

Delicious eaten cold, stuffed in pitta breads or wraps for next day's lunch.

If the thought of rinsing baked beans horrifies you, use a tin of any white beans – haricot, borlotti and cannelini all work well. But honestly, it's just a bit of tomato sauce.

GIGANTES PLAKI

Gigantes Plaki literally means 'Really Big Beans'! I'm heading back to my Mediterranean roots with this simple but delicious dish. I can have it for dinner, then lunch the next day and pulse any leftovers into a soup. It makes me chuckle to see these spicy butterbeans retailing for almost £5 per pot in certain supermarkets, when they're really just bigger, better baked beans. You can either soak dried beans overnight in cold water – which means they will need to be drained, rinsed and boiled vigorously for 10 minutes separately to the sauce in order to get rid of any toxins – or use a tin of ready-prepared butter beans, which is more expensive but more convenient. If cooking with dried butter beans, use only 150g. I like to serve this dish with rice and green beans as a vegetarian meal, or it is great with baked chicken or fish.

Serves 2

1 onion

1 clove of garlic

a splash of oil

a pinch of ground cinnamon

1 x 400g carton or tin of chopped tomatoes

½ a bunch of fresh basil, plus extra to garnish

a splash of lemon juice

1 x 400g tin of butter beans, drained and rinsed

1 vegetable stock cube

75g Greek cheese
(such as feta), crumbled

Finely chop the onion and garlic and put into a large saucepan along with the oil and cinnamon. Cook on a low heat until the onion is softened, then add the chopped tomatoes and continue to simmer on a low heat for a few more minutes.

Chop all the basil stalks. Add the lemon juice, chopped basil stalks and the basil leaves (leaving the extra basil aside for a garnish) and stir in, continuing to simmer.

Stir in the butter beans and crumble in the vegetable stock cube, with a little water if necessary. Stir well to dissolve. Simmer all together on a low heat for approximately 20 minutes.

Ladle into bowls and serve garnished with the crumbled cheese and remaining basil leaves.

TIPS: Gigantes Plaki can also be eaten cold as a mezze or snack, or mixed with leftover rice and stuffed into a pitta bread for next day's lunch – it's delicious cold and perfectly portable.

If you don't have any basil, this is also very good made with parsley.

You can make fab burgers from this mixture. Just strain off the tomato sauce, crush and add an extra clove of garlic and a pinch of dried chilli flakes, then gently mash the beans and shape into burgers with floured hands. Fry for a few minutes on each side.

PEACH AND CHICKPEA CURRY

This is my favourite curry, my go-to, easy but perfect comfort food. I used to make it with turkey but now I use chickpeas instead so it's a deliciously wholesomely vegan dish. Serve this gorgeous fruity curry with simple plain boiled rice.

Serves 2 (for dinner, with enough leftovers for lunch)

250g tinned chickpeas (drained weight)

1 onion

1 clove of garlic

1 chilli

a splash of oil

a shake of ground cumin

1 x 400g tin of peaches

1 x 400g carton or tin of chopped tomatoes

a handful of fresh coriander, finely chopped

1 vegetable stock cube

Drain your chickpeas and rinse them vigorously to get rid of the stagnant water that they'll have been sitting in. Pop them in some fresh water in a saucepan and boil rapidly for a good 10 minutes to remove any toxins.

Meanwhile, peel and finely chop the onion and garlic, and chop the chilli. Put the oil into another saucepan and add the onion, garlic and chilli, then the cumin, and cook gently on a low heat. Allow the onions to sweat, not brown. If they burn, the burnt taste will permeate through your whole curry, whereas sweating them will add a delicious sweetness.

Drain the peaches, reserving the juice, and chop into small chunks. Add to the onion mixture in the pan, along with any juice from the tin. By this time, the chickpeas should have finished vigorously boiling, so reduce them down to a simmer (or take off the heat if using tinned chickpeas).

Pour the chopped tomatoes over the peaches and onion, add the coriander and crumble in the stock cube. Then stir everything together. Reduce the heat to a low setting, and allow to cook gently for at least 30 minutes. This thickens the sauce and melds the flavours together – if chopped finely enough, the onions will disappear as they thicken the sauce with a sweet spiciness. You may need to add a cup of water to the sauce if it starts to get too thick. Drain and rinse the chickpeas and tip into the sauce. Stir, then serve.

TIPS: This keeps in the fridge for 2 to 3 days and freezes well. Leftovers can be served in a pitta bread for a delicious lunch.

For a hearty meaty version, add cooked turkey or lamb to the curry along with the chickpeas. If using turkey, pre-roast a large drumstick and just peel the meat off the bone. Or fry some diced lamb (a cheap cut will do) and add that to the pan.

A few of my readers have emailed me to say that they add different spices, or cheap curry powder, or a handful of sultanas as variations – and this is a great dish to smuggle in any leftover vegetables.

SMOKY RED LENTIL BURGERS

These are a favourite of mine, especially for impressing veggie friends. The lentils need to be cooked until they are almost translucent and falling apart, but they will firm up again as they cool down later on. You can add a sliced chilli or a pinch of dried chilli flakes to the mixture for an extra kick, depending on how adventurous you are. The burgers are delicious in a bun or pitta bread with home-made tzatziki (or natural yoghurt mixed with lemon, parsley and coriander). Alternatively, serve with boiled rice through which you've stirred lemon juice and chopped fresh coriander, and some green beans on the side.

Makes 4 chunky burgers

100g dried red lentils, rinsed

1 onion

1 fat clove of garlic

1 carrot

1–2 tablespoons oil, plus extra to fry the burgers

2 teaspoons paprika

a splash of lemon juice

1 slice of bread or a pitta bread (this is a good way to use up stale bread)

optional: 1 egg, beaten

1 heaped tablespoon flour, plus extra for shaping the burgers

fresh coriander, to serve

Bring a small saucepan of water to the boil and put in the lentils. Cook on a medium heat for 10 minutes. Once softened, remove the lentils from the heat and drain. Stir them with a spoon or fork in order to make sure all the excess water drains away and set to one side. Keep the now-empty saucepan for the next stage.

Peel and finely chop the onion and garlic, and wash and grate the carrot, and put them all into the small saucepan along with the oil. Add the paprika and lemon juice, and cook gently on a low to medium heat until the onions have softened.

Tip the lentils back into the pan, and remove from the heat. Grate the bread into the pan and mix everything together well. Add the egg (see tip below for how to make the burgers without the egg) and the flour to bind the mixture together.

Once thoroughly cooled – around half an hour later – form into patties by shaping a heaped tablespoon or two of the mixture in floured hands. Fry the burgers in a splash of oil for around 5 minutes on each side – handling with care as they may be a bit fragile. When golden and slightly crisp on the outsides they are ready. Chop the coriander and serve the burgers with a little sprinkled on top.

TIPS: For vegans, or for a lower-cost burger, omit the egg, but allow the mixture to cool for longer to firm up and bind together, and ensure that it doesn't fall apart when cooking.

Instead of making burgers, shape some of the mixture into balls and shallow fry like falafels. These can be taken to work or school for lunch, eaten cold from the fridge, or in pitta breads with a little salad and mayonnaise or mango chutney.

The patties can be stored uncooked in the fridge overnight, or frozen individually for up to 3 months. Cooked burgers can also be individually stored in the freezer for up to 3 months.

WARM SPICY DAAL

There are many different recipes for daal, made with different types of split peas, lentils and even chickpeas, so here is a simple basic one to get you started. From here, feel free to customize to your own taste by adding plain yoghurt, coconut yoghurt or different herbs and spices. I like to eat mine from a deep bowl with a toasted pitta bread or two – or a naan bread if you can stretch to that.

Serves 3

100g dried red lentils

1 onion

1 teaspoon ground cumin

a splash of oil

1 chicken stock cube, dissolved in 1 litre boiling water

1 x 400g carton or tin of chopped tomatoes

1 tablespoon chopped fresh coriander, plus extra to serve

Rinse the lentils in cold water and drain. Place in a saucepan, cover with fresh water and bring to the boil, skimming off any scum that rises with a spoon.

Meanwhile, peel and chop the onion into small pieces and place in a small frying pan with the cumin and oil. Fry gently for a few minutes to release the spice's flavour and soften the onion. Then add to the saucepan containing the lentils along with the stock, chopped tomatoes and coriander. Reduce to a low heat and simmer for 20 minutes, or until the lentils are swollen. Check towards the end of cooking and add a little more water if required.

Stir well, then serve garnished with more chopped coriander.

TIPS: If you've got some, use natural yoghurt instead of the chopped tomatoes and substitute ground turmeric for the ground cumin for a rich, sweet, creamier-tasting version.

Delicious with frozen spinach, lemon and yoghurt in place of the chopped tomatoes, and great cold for lunch in a pitta bread, too.

HUMMUS

I love hummus. I make it plain, like the recipe below, or add caramelized onion slices or a grilled and crushed tomato with a little spinach or a generous shake of spice. Traditional hummus recipes use expensive tahini paste – but I've never bothered. If I want that nutty, cloying taste, I add a heaped teaspoon of peanut butter instead. The quantities given below are for a whole large tin of chickpeas – because you can never have too much hummus!

Makes 1 large bowl to share

1 x 400g tin of chickpeas

zest and juice of 1 lemon or 2 tablespoons bottled lemon juice

2 tablespoons oil

2 cloves of garlic, peeled and finely chopped

a generous shake of paprika or ground cumin

Drain and rinse the chickpeas, then pop them into a small saucepan of water. Bring to the boil and reduce to a simmer for 10 minutes to soften.

When softened, drain the chickpeas and tip back into the saucepan with a couple of tablespoons of the cooking water, the lemon zest and juice, oil and garlic. Mash everything vigorously with a fork or masher, adding a little extra water if you need to.

Serve with the paprika or cumin sprinkled on top, and enjoy.

TIP: This will keep in the fridge, covered, for up to 2 days. If it starts to harden, stir a splash of water through to loosen it up, and a dash of lemon juice to refresh it.

TAKE A PACKET OF PASTA . . .

Pasta is my 'junk' food, my fast and easy filling dinner or versatile lunch, which can be as simple as pouring a carton of chopped tomatoes on top with a shake of dried mixed herbs, or as quick as stirring it into leftover soup.

There are many different kinds of pasta out there – I keep spaghetti and penne pasta in the cupboard, both of which are stocked in most supermarket value ranges. Spaghetti is good for thinner sauces like Best-o Pesto (see page 84) or with leftover soup, whereas penne works well with chunky dishes, like the Creamy Greek Cheese and Courgette Pasta (see page 98) or Macaroni Peas (see page 99). If you have a packet of pasta in the cupboard and a basil plant on the windowsill, then you always have an emergency meal to hand. Add a carton of chopped tomatoes and it's practically haute cuisine. Practically.

USE-ME-FOR-ANYTHING TOMATO SAUCE

This tomato sauce is exactly what its name says – a wonderfully versatile sauce for all occasions. It was inspired by a basic tomato sauce in *Economy Gastronomy* by Allegra McEvedy and Paul Merrett – which is a brilliant guide to cooking fantastic food on a budget. I make a batch, then eat some, fridge some and freeze the rest for later. The quantities given here make 6 small portions.

Serves 4–6

2 tablespoons oil

1 onion, peeled and chopped

2 cloves of garlic, peeled and finely chopped

1 small red chilli, chopped and deseeded, or a pinch of chilli flakes

2 tablespoons red wine or red wine vinegar (optional)

2 x 400g tins of chopped tomatoes

2 tablespoons tomato purée or tomato ketchup

Heat the oil in a saucepan and add the chopped onion. Stir in the garlic and chilli and cook on a medium heat until the onions are translucent and sweet.

Measure the wine or wine vinegar into the pan and stir for a few minutes on a low heat until the pungent alcohol or vinegary smell is no longer as strong. Then add the remaining ingredients to the pan – the chopped tomatoes and tomato purée or ketchup. Cook gently, stirring occasionally, for 20 minutes, by which time the sauce should be thickened and glossy.

Remove from the heat and serve, or divide into portions and either put into the fridge or cool and freeze.

TIPS: I usually eat some immediately over 75g of cooked spaghetti, refrigerate a portion for the next day and freeze the remainder in Tupperware and ice cube trays for a quick meal for Small Boy.

This sauce is also delicious with some grated courgette stirred in, served with fish like pilchards, anchovies, chunks of trout or any baked white fish.

Use as the base for a sort-of ratatouille, by adding any veg from the bottom of the fridge or freezer drawer.

For a lovely savoury flavour, try making this sauce with 8 anchovies broken into chunks, 1 tablespoon of sliced black olives and a handful of chopped fresh basil stirred in at the end. Use half the quantity of chopped tomatoes and omit the vinegar and tomato purée.

BEST-O PESTO

I love making my own pesto – freshly chopped basil leaves with a generous sprinkling of finely grated cheese easily beat anything I can buy in the supermarket. I use a mixture of half basil leaves and half parsley, and just 'ordinary' oil. This is a basic recipe, so feel free to leave out the garlic, add ground nuts, use olive oil if you have it, and play around. Pasta simply dressed by tossing with home-made pesto really is the best easy lunch or dinner dish!

Makes 1 small jar (serves 4)

a large fistful of fresh basil

a large fistful of fresh parsley

2 cloves of garlic

50g hard strong cheese

100ml sunflower or vegetable oil

First, finely chop the herbs together. I put mine into a mug or small bowl and chop into them with kitchen scissors, but you can chop them finely on a chopping board if you like. Peel and finely chop or crush the garlic and add it to the herbs in the bowl. Grate in the cheese. Pour over the oil, stir well and that's all there is to it.

Once made, you can keep the pesto for a week in a sealed jar in the fridge, or freeze in an ice cube tray and pop a cube out whenever you fancy a quick lunch.

TIPS: Serve warm tossed with new potatoes, pasta and green beans for a speedy winter Pasta alla Genovese (see page 94).

For a posher pesto, add 1 very finely chopped chilli and some finely chopped black olives.

For a zingy fresh mint pesto, replace the basil with mint in the above recipe and add a squeeze of lemon juice.

To make a winter pesto, replace the basil with rosemary or thyme.

ONION PASTA WITH PARSLEY AND RED WINE

I always buy a dozen onions at a time, as these hardy little vegetables keep for over a week in the fridge and form the base for most of my savoury recipes. However, sometimes I seem to end up with a few too many – in which case, I turn them into a delicious meal in their own right, such as this recipe.

Serves 2

2 onions

1 tablespoon oil

160g pasta or spaghetti

4 tablespoons red wine

a handful of fresh parsley, finely chopped

2 tablespoons grated hard strong cheese

Peel and finely slice the onions, and place in a frying pan with the oil on a low heat to cook slowly. Meanwhile, bring a medium saucepan of water to the boil and put in the pasta. Cook according to the packet instructions, usually 8 to 10 minutes.

As the onions start to soften, add 2 tablespoons of the red wine and stir in, turning the heat up to medium. When the wine has been absorbed, add the remaining 2 tablespoons.

Once the pasta is cooked, drain and toss with the onions. Serve with generous amounts of parsley and cheese scattered on top.

TIP: This dish uses very similar ingredients to the recipe for Onion Soup with Red Wine (see page 55), so you can always buy in bulk and make both together.

MUSHROOM AND SPINACH PASTA

This came about as most of my recipes do, with a frantic head looking in the fridge and a 'Hmm, what am I going to do with those tired mushrooms?' One of my hero ingredients is frozen spinach, but handfuls of the fresh stuff work just as well here. This dish may not sound fancy, but it's one of my favourites so far. I find it's therapeutic to go at the herbs and spinach with scissors at the end of a working day – this also saves my poor worktop. I like my cooking to be physical and de-stressing, as well as cheap, simple and nutritious!

Serves 2

150g spaghetti

1 onion

1 clove of garlic

a splash of oil

a splash of lemon juice

100g mushrooms

a fistful of fresh parsley

a fistful of thyme

70g frozen spinach, defrosted and squeezed of excess water, or a few generous fistfuls of the fresh stuff

30g hard strong cheese, grated

Break the spaghetti in half and put into a saucepan of water. Bring to the boil.

Peel and finely chop the onion and garlic. Put into a separate saucepan or small sauté pan with the oil and lemon juice, and cook gently over a low heat until translucent. Gently clean any excess earth from the mushrooms with a clean tea towel and break them up by hand, then add to the pan.

Finely chop the herbs and spinach together. I put mine into a bowl and go at it all with scissors. Drain the pasta and toss with the spinach, herbs, mushrooms, onion and garlic, along with any juices from the mushroom pan. Serve in two bowls, scatter the cheese on top and enjoy.

TIPS: My non-vegan friends would love this served with shavings of Parmesan on top, or some crumbled goat's cheese or chunks of Brie, and on all three counts I would be highly jealous of them!

For the carnivores among you, add some scraps of cooked bacon for a seriously sensational dinner.

CARROT RIBBON PASTA

This recipe is best made with long pasta like spaghetti or, if you're feeling fancy, tagliatelle or fettuccine would be delightful. Use a vegetable peeler to cut the carrot into long ribbons to toss with the pasta. You can top this with Use-Me-For-Anything Tomato Sauce (see page 83) for a heartier dinner, or eat it cold the next day for lunch. Play with this dish – add peas for a colourful display or grate lemon zest over and scatter some parsley on top to serve. It's also delicious with some crumbled feta stirred through, although I like the simple version below best of all.

Serves 2

150g spaghetti

2 large carrots (the longer the better)

a handful of fresh basil

a handful of fresh parsley

a handful of grated hard strong cheese, to taste

30ml oil

zest and juice of ½ a lemon or 1 tablespoon bottled lemon juice

First, put a saucepan of water on to boil, and pop the pasta in to cook according to the packet instructions (usually 8 to 10 minutes). Meanwhile wash the carrots, then, using a vegetable peeler, strip each into long, thin ribbons. A couple of minutes before the pasta is done, pop the carrot ribbons into the pot.

In a separate dish or tea cup, finely chop the basil and parsley and add the grated cheese. Pour in the oil and lemon juice, grate over the lemon zest and mix well to combine the sauce.

When the pasta and carrot ribbons are cooked, drain thoroughly. Tip back into the saucepan and toss well with the sauce to combine.

Serve and devour.

TIP: For a cold, sweet summer salad, add a handful of sultanas or some grated apple tossed in a little lemon juice to stop it from browning. My son loves 'rainbow pasta' for his lunch.

CAR-BRIE-NARA

My take on the classic spaghetti carbonara recipe uses value range Brie in place of expensive Parmesan, to give a creamy, luxurious sauce that perfectly complements the salty tang of bacon. It takes just minutes to knock together, and has Small Boy asking me to make it again and again. Quantities are approximate, so if you have too little bacon or too much Brie, don't worry too much about it – it's hard to go wrong with this one.

Serves 2

160g spaghetti

1 onion

1 fat clove of garlic or ½ a teaspoon of the dried stuff

120g bacon (the streakier the better)

juice of ½ a lemon or 2 teaspoons bottled lemon juice

50g Brie cheese

a handful of fresh parsley or 1 teaspoon dried mixed herbs, plus extra to garnish

200ml natural yoghurt or double cream

First, bring a medium saucepan of water to the boil and pop the pasta in. Reduce the heat to a medium simmer and cook according to packet instructions, normally 8 to 10 minutes.

Meanwhile, as the pasta is cooking, peel and finely slice the onion and garlic, and place in a frying pan or sauté pan. Chop the bacon into small pieces and add to the pan, squeezing the lemon juice over. Put on a very low heat to allow the fat to seep from the bacon, which will be what you cook the garlic and onion in, and cook gently for a few minutes until the onion has softened, stirring to seal the bacon on all sides. Chop the Brie into cubes. When there is a layer of fat in the pan, toss in the Brie, and turn the heat up to medium.

Chop the parsley and add to the pan with the yoghurt or cream. Stir in to heat through. Drain the pasta, add to the pan, and stir well to coat in the bacony-cheesy sauce. Serve in bowls with extra parsley to garnish.

TIPS: Add mushrooms to bulk it out a bit, or in place of the bacon if you are a vegetarian – in which case, you need to add a tablespoon of oil to cook them in.

This will keep well in the fridge for 2 to 3 days, making it an ideal make-ahead dish for lunches. Delicious reheated or eaten cold.

LEMONY SPINACH PASTA WITH BROWN LENTILS

I love lentils – they're cheap, filling and versatile – but I didn't discover them until a couple of years ago. Originally writing them off as 'strange and healthy', curiosity eventually got the better of me and now these feature frequently in my weekly shop. Here I've mixed them with a few other familiar ingredients – pasta, natural yoghurt and frozen spinach – for a versatile lunch or dinner dish.

Serves 2

1 fat clove of garlic

1 small red chilli

a fistful of fresh parsley

70g frozen spinach, defrosted and squeezed of excess water

zest and juice of 1 lemon or 2 tablespoons bottled lemon juice

2 tablespoons oil

a pinch of salt

50g dried brown lentils

150g pasta

3 tablespoons natural yoghurt

Peel the garlic and crush or very finely chop into a teacup or small bowl. Finely chop the chilli, parsley and spinach, add them to the bowl and grate over the lemon zest. Add the oil, squeeze in the lemon juice, and finish with a pinch of salt. Mix well together.

Bring a saucepan of water to the boil and put in the brown lentils. Cook for 10 to 12 minutes then add the pasta and cook both together for a further 8 to 10 minutes (or according to the packet instructions). The lentils need to cook for 20 minutes in total.

When the pasta and lentils are done, drain well. Stir the yoghurt into the spinach mixture to make the sauce, and stir through the pasta. Serve warm or cold.

TIPS: Any leftovers can be kept for next day's lunch, if allowed to cool and kept covered in the fridge.

Kale is a great, versatile, easy-to-grow leaf that would make a delicious substitute for spinach in this dish.

ONION, CABBAGE AND CHEESE PASTA

I use a Savoy cabbage for this dish, which can be chopped and frozen to make it last beyond the few leaves needed here, or bought in frozen bags from most supermarkets. However, any green cabbage will do. Similarly, you can substitute pretty much any cheese for the Brie or hard strong cheese – I have even sometimes thrown a chopped up mini Babybel into this, and it still works brilliantly.

Serves 2

2 tablespoons vegetable oil

1 large onion

1 clove of garlic

2–4 large Savoy cabbage leaves

1 tablespoon flour

100ml milk

50g Brie or hard strong cheese

140g pasta

First, put the pasta water on to boil at the back of the stove. Then put 1 tablespoon of the oil into a medium-sized saucepan. Peel and finely chop the onion, and peel and crush or finely chop the garlic. Add them all to the pan on a low heat, stirring every now and again.

Cut the thick stem away from the middle of the cabbage leaves, shred finely, and add to the saucepan. When the vegetables have softened, tip into a bowl to one side and keep for later.

Add the pasta to the now-boiling water and cook for 8 to 10 minutes (or according to the packet instructions).

While the pasta cooks, make the cheesy sauce using the same saucepan from the vegetables. Put in the remaining 1 tablespoon of oil and the flour and stir together quickly over a medium heat to make a paste. Add a little milk and stir constantly with a wooden spoon or a fork to make a smooth sauce. Keep adding the milk little by little and stirring all the time until you have a sauce of medium thickness.

Grate or chop the cheese into cubes and add to the sauce. Tip the cooked vegetables back into the sauce and stir until the cheese has melted.

Drain the pasta and serve with the sauce on top. Enjoy!

TIPS: Try this with a leek in place of the onion and, if your budget will stretch to smoked cheese, that is delicious instead of the Brie or hard strong cheese.

To make this dish vegan, omit the cheese and use soya milk in place of the milk. Add the vegetables to the white sauce with a splash of lemon and allow to cook for longer on a lower heat to infuse the flavours together.

If you're a carnivore, this would be delicious with some cubes of bacon cooked in with the vegetables at the beginning.

SUMMER PASTA ALLA GENOVESE

I use courgettes liberally in my cooking in the summer, as they are cheaper at that time of year. They are one of my 'hero' ingredients: courgettes are a good source of fibre, vitamin A and vitamin C, and can be smuggled into most dishes without small children (or fussy grown-ups) noticing. Here, I make a simple, versatile courgette and mint pesto that can be eaten with pasta on its own or, as below, tossed with little peas and al dente broccoli for a delicious and healthy pasta dinner. You can also make the pesto in a bigger batch and freeze it in ice cube trays for later use.

Serves 2

160g pasta

a handful of fresh mint or
1 teaspoon dried mint

a handful of fresh basil or
1 teaspoon dried basil, plus extra
to serve

1 large courgette, stalk
and end removed

zest and juice of 1 lemon or
2 tablespoons bottled lemon
juice, plus extra to serve

a splash of oil

optional: 30g hard strong cheese

70g broccoli

70g frozen peas

optional: black pepper, to serve

Bring a medium-sized saucepan of water to the boil and put in the pasta. Simmer on a medium heat until the pasta is cooked, usually around 8 to 10 minutes (or according to the packet instructions).

Meanwhile, make the courgette pesto. Chop the mint and basil together in a mug or small bowl. Grate in the courgette – including the skin – then add the lemon zest and juice and the oil. Finely grate in the cheese, if you are using it, and mix everything together.

Chop the broccoli into thumb-sized pieces, or larger if you prefer, but remember the larger pieces will take longer to cook. Shortly before the pasta has finished cooking, add the broccoli to the saucepan along with the frozen peas, and let the vegetables cook for 1 to 2 minutes in with the pasta before removing the pan from the boil.

Drain the pasta and vegetables, add the pesto and toss together to coat. Serve with extra basil and lemon juice, and black pepper to taste, if using.

TIPS: For a little kick, add a finely chopped chilli to the grated courgette pesto.

To make a creamy sauce, add a few tablespoons of natural yoghurt to the courgette pesto.

For a winter version, use 200g potatoes and 70g fine green beans, both cut into 2cm chunks/pieces, instead of the broccoli and peas. In place of the courgette and lemon zest and juice in the pesto sauce, use 1 small crushed clove of garlic, 4 tablespoons oil and the 30g grated hard strong cheese, plus a splash of the vegetable cooking water.

ROMAN PASTA WITH MANDARINS AND A CREAMY BASIL SAUCE

This dish is inspired by a recipe in Sarah Raven's *Garden Cookbook*. My copy is a very well-thumbed and now very grubby book that has been much loved and often read. I picked it up in a second-hand shop a year or so ago and could not understand for the life of me why someone would have given it away. Packed with stunning photographs and beautifully simple food, I read it from cover to cover like a novel and took many of the recipes to heart. This was the first time I had heard of the idea of using oranges with pasta – apparently a treat in Rome – and adapted it to use tinned mandarins and natural yoghurt. It is a quick spring and summer staple in my house and friends are always surprised at just how delicious it is.

Serves 2

1 large onion

2 tablespoons oil

150g pasta

a handful of fresh basil, plus extra to serve

a handful of fresh parsley, plus extra to serve

200g tinned mandarins (approximate drained weight)

200ml natural yoghurt

grated hard strong cheese, to serve

Peel and finely slice the onion, and toss into a frying pan. Add the oil and sweat the onions on a medium heat.

Meanwhile, bring a saucepan of water to the boil and pop the pasta in. Cook according to packet instructions, normally around 8 to 10 minutes for dried pasta.

Finely chop the basil and parsley, and add to the pan with the onions. Using a spoon to drain off most of the juice, add the mandarins to the pan and stir in. When the onions have softened, remove from the heat and pour in the yoghurt, mixing it through with a wooden spoon.

Drain the pasta and toss with the sauce. Serve with a generous amount of grated cheese, and extra chopped basil and parsley.

CREAMY GREEK CHEESE AND COURGETTE PASTA

This classic combination of Greek cheese and courgettes crops up again in a simple pasta dish that is perfect for lunch all year round. Eat cold in the summer, or warmed through in the winter to melt the cheese into a soft, delicious sauce.

Serves 2

1 courgette

a fistful of fresh mint, plus extra to garnish

a fistful of fresh parsley

1 tablespoon oil

zest and juice of ½ a lemon or 1 tablespoon bottled lemon juice

1 clove of garlic, peeled

50g Greek cheese (goat's cheese or feta)

100ml natural yoghurt, plus a little extra to taste

160g pasta

70g fresh or frozen green beans, trimmed

Preheat the oven to 180°C/350°F/gas 4.

Chop off the stalk and end from the courgette. Dice and toss into a shallow roasting tin. Pop the mint and parsley into a tea-cup and chop finely with kitchen scissors. Pour the oil over the herbs, add the grated lemon zest, squeeze in the juice and press in the garlic. Stir well and pour over the courgette in the roasting tin, shaking to coat it in the mixture. Pop the dish into the preheated oven for 30 to 40 minutes to roast.

When the courgette is cooked, tip out into a bowl, pouring in all of the juices from the roasting tin. Crumble the cheese over the roasted courgette, and mash roughly with a fork. Stir in the yoghurt, and set to one side.

Bring a pot of water to the boil and put in the pasta. Cook according to the packet instructions – usually simmering for around 8 to 10 minutes. After about 4 or 5 minutes, add the green beans to the pot, crank the heat up and cook them in with the pasta until soft but still a vibrant green.

Drain the pasta and green beans, and tip in the cheesy courgette sauce in. Mix well to coat, adding extra yoghurt if you want a runnier sauce. Serve in deep comforting bowls, with additional mint leaves to garnish.

TIP: If you are short of time or don't want to use the electricity/gas for roasting, simply grate the courgette instead of dicing it, mix with the rest of the roasting marinade ingredients and let them sit together whilst the pasta cooks. The flavour will be less intense but still utterly delicious – and super quick!

MACARONI PEAS

This recipe is based on one from Hugh Fearnley-Whittingstall's *River Cottage Veg Every Day!* cookbook and was sent to me by a reader who recommended it for its simplicity and goodness. I normally add a handful of mint to mine and a squeeze of lemon juice to lift it. I detested peas as a child, but will eat this by the bowlful.

Serves 2

150g macaroni or penne pasta

1 clove of garlic

1 onion

25g butter or 2 tablespoons oil

150g frozen petits pois

a handful of fresh parsley, plus extra to serve

30g hard strong cheese, plus extra to serve

Bring a saucepan of water to the boil. Reduce to a simmer, add the pasta and cook according to the packet instructions, normally around 8 to 10 minutes.

Meanwhile, make the sauce. Peel and finely chop or crush the garlic, and peel and finely chop the onion. Heat the butter or oil in a medium non-stick saucepan, put the onion and garlic into the pan and cook gently for a couple of minutes on a low heat.

Add the peas to the onion and garlic and cook until tender, but still a vivid green. Test one by squashing it between finger and thumb – if it yields easily then it's done. Remove a third of the peas into a bowl (don't worry if you get some onion and garlic in there too) and set to one side.

Put the rest of the peas, onion and garlic into a blender with the parsley and a few tablespoons of the cooking water from the pasta. Grate in the cheese and blend. The sauce should be smooth but not too runny.

Drain the pasta and toss with the hot pea sauce and reserved whole peas. Garnish with extra grated cheese and chopped parsley to serve.

OR A BAG OF RICE . . .

Rice comes in so many different varieties – Arborio, paella, wild, pudding, even red and purple – that it could be easy to think that you need to use them all in order to cook good rice-based meals. However, although these varieties all have different qualities, they are 'nice to have' rather than essential. I keep a bag of value range long-grain rice in the cupboard and I use it in everything I cook – from Garlic and Parsley Risotto (see page 104) and Sort-of Paella (see page 111) to Avgolemono (see page 57). I even cook long-grain rice with a dash of milk and sultanas for a quick rice pudding. (see my blog agirlcalledjack.com for the recipe.)

The trick to a good rice dish is not about having several different varieties in the cupboard, it's what you do with the one you have that counts. I'm proud to say that I can make a great risotto from the common little long grain. Risotto purists everywhere will be horrified, I'm sure, but it works for me.

BRIE AND BACON RISOTTO

This was an inevitable concoction made from some leftover ingredients in my fridge, as I always find the packs of bacon that I buy have large chunks in plus some scrappy bits, and until I came up with this recipe I was at a loss what to do with them. If in doubt, make leftover bacon scraps into a risotto – or my easy, quick version of risotto, that is. Brie is often considered a 'posh cheese' – and perhaps a surprising recommendation on a limited budget, but the value range is extremely inexpensive and still gives a rich flavour and creamy versatility. I find a hunk of Brie far more satisfying for my stomach and my wallet than plain old Cheddar any day.

Serves 2

150g bacon

1 red or white onion

180g rice

1 chicken stock cube, dissolved in 500ml boiling water

60g Brie cheese

a handful of chopped fresh parsley

optional: cranberry sauce or apple sauce, to serve

Chop the bacon into small pieces – approximately 1cm square. Place in a colander and thoroughly rinse under cold water to remove some of the salty taste.

Put the bacon into a shallow frying or sauté pan. Peel and finely chop the onion, and add to the pan. Bring the pan up to a low heat. No additional fat is required: the fat will 'leak' from the bacon as it heats slowly, so make the most of it! Soften the onion in the bacon fat and when it's almost translucent, add the rice and stir in well to coat the edges.

When the ends of the grains of rice have started to turn clear, add half of the stock to the pan and stir in. Let the rice cook and absorb that amount of liquid, then keep adding the remaining stock gradually, a little at a time, as it is absorbed by the rice. You may find that you do not need all of the stock – a good risotto should have a soupy texture, but be slightly al dente.

Just before serving, chop the Brie and stir through until it is mostly melted. Scatter the parsley on top to lift the flavour. If you have any apple or cranberry sauce kicking around in the cupboard, a teaspoon swirled through the risotto would be divine.

TIPS: Substitute a blue cheese for the Brie – most supermarkets will have a value range Stilton-style cheese for far less than its authentic counterparts but which is still delicious!

Mushrooms work well instead of bacon for a vegetarian alternative, although you'll need to add a splash of oil when cooking the onion.

Leftover risotto can be eaten the next day, either warmed through, or as a cold rice salad for lunch.

GARLIC AND PARSLEY RISOTTO

Plain white rice is just as good as risotto rice in this dish. White rice is white rice, and here it is simply a vehicle for pungent, sweet flavours. If you have Arborio rice, feel free to use it, but I save that for very special occasions these days. I eat this simple risotto from a bowl, soupy and delicious, sometimes with sausages, sometimes with chicken, and sometimes with a handful of mushrooms stirred in and topped with grated hard strong cheese.

Serves 4

1 bulb of garlic (yes, really!)

2 tablespoons oil

1 onion

400g rice

100ml white wine

a generous handful of chopped fresh parsley

hard strong cheese, to serve

Preheat the oven to 180°C/350°F/gas 4.

First, roast the garlic. Chop the root and stalk ends from the bulb, split it into cloves and place the unpeeled cloves in a roasting tin with 1 tablespoon of the oil. Some folks roast garlic in its papery skin, some don't. I'm in the papery skin camp, simply because I love to squish it out with my fingers when it's soft and sweet. Pop the roasting tin into the preheated oven for 20 minutes. Alternatively, peel the cloves, rub with the oil and place in a microwaveable dish. Microwave on medium power for 5 minutes for a quick and easy way to roast garlic without the need for an oven.

Peel and slice the onion, and place in a large frying or sauté pan with the remaining 1 tablespoon of oil. Soften on a medium heat. When the onions are almost translucent, pour in the rice and stir well for a minute. When the ends of the rice have started to turn transparent, add the wine and stir.

Once the wine is absorbed, add half a cup of boiling water and stir. Continue adding boiling water, half a cup at a time, until the rice is cooked and the risotto soupy.

Remove the garlic from the oven and squeeze the sweet roasted pulp from the cloves into the risotto. Stir it through along with the parsley, and serve the risotto with some hard strong cheese grated over the top.

PEA AND MINT RISOTTO

To make this dish of ricy goodness even more delicious, stir in some scraps of cooking bacon along with the sliced onion, squeeze over a little lemon juice at the end of cooking or sprinkle a generous pile of grated hard strong cheese over the top of each bowl just before serving.

Serves 2

1 onion

2 tablespoons oil

140g rice

30ml white wine

1 vegetable stock cube, dissolved in 500ml boiling water

a fistful of fresh mint

a fistful of fresh parsley

100g frozen petits pois

Peel and finely slice the onion and put into a sauté pan with the oil over a low heat. Once the onion has softened, add the rice and stir for a couple of minutes until the edges start to turn translucent. Pour over the wine and a little of the stock, and stir in, allowing the rice to absorb the liquid.

Keep adding the stock a little at a time and stirring, stirring, stirring. People pretend that making risotto is hard, but as long as you keep it on a low heat, add stock when it starts to dry out, and stir it a lot, you'll be fine!

Finely chop the herbs in a tea cup or small bowl with kitchen scissors and add most of them to the pan. Keep some to one side for a garnish.

When the rice is al dente (slightly crunchy but edible) or softer depending on personal preference, stir in the peas. Cook until the peas are tender, then remove the pan from the heat and spoon into bowls. Garnish with the reserved chopped herbs.

EARTHY RED WINE AND MUSHROOM RISOTTO

When I need easy but comforting food, I always turn to a large bowl of warm, flavourful rice – and using red wine as a base works beautifully. In the winter, serve this risotto in a deep bowl with a spoon, whilst snuggling under a thick blanket. Or it can make a special meal for two served with some lovely crusty bread, if you're so inclined. You could also eat this risotto as a side dish with roasted chicken thighs or sausages, but I eat mine by itself with some green vegetables on the side.

Serves 2 as a side dish or
1 as a main meal

1 teaspoon oil

1 clove of garlic

100g mushrooms

1 teaspoon dried mixed herbs or a fistful of chopped fresh thyme and parsley, plus extra to taste

140g rice

75ml red wine

1 tablespoon tomato purée

1 vegetable stock cube, dissolved in 700ml boiling water

Heat the oil gently in a frying pan. Peel and finely slice the garlic and add to the pan. Gently clean any excess earth from the mushrooms with a clean tea towel, chop them into small chunks and add to the pan. Shake the herbs over and allow everything to cook together for a few minutes to sauté the garlic and mushrooms.

Add the rice and stir to coat in the oil. When the rice starts to turn translucent, pour in the wine and add the tomato purée, stirring constantly to prevent any of the rice sticking to the pan.

When the wine is almost all absorbed, start to add the stock, one ladleful at a time. Stir in each time until almost all the liquid has been absorbed and then add another ladleful of stock. Repeat until either the stock is gone or the rice is cooked to your liking.

Sprinkle on some additional herbs to taste and serve.

TIP: This recipe uses almost the same ingredients as the Red Wine and Mushroom Soup (see page 51), so you could make them both at the same time.

COURGETTE, TOMATO AND BRIE GRATIN

This dish was born of a sad-looking courgette in my fridge, half of a very large onion that was starting to dry out and some bits and pieces from my cupboard. The rice makes this filling and comforting, and the cheese, tomato and slightly crisp courgettes have me reaching for the second portion even when I am pleasantly full. If you have always been a bit disdainful about courgettes, this simple supper might just change your mind. You can double the recipe quantities to make one big gratin to serve 4 people – in which case use a roasting tin rather than individual ovenproof dishes.

Serves 2

1 onion

150g rice

1 chicken or vegetable stock cube, dissolved in 200ml boiling water

1 x 400g carton or tin of chopped tomatoes

a few sprigs of fresh basil

a few sprigs of fresh parsley

1 courgette

50g Brie cheese or to taste

a drizzle of oil, plus extra to grease the ovenproof dishes

Preheat the oven to 180°C/350°F/gas 4.

First, peel and dice the onion and put into a sauté pan or frying pan along with the rice. Pour in the stock a little at a time, on a low heat, stirring frequently until each addition is absorbed and then adding the next. You may need to add more or less liquid until the rice is just cooked, but boiling water to top up will be fine if you run out of stock.

Add the chopped tomatoes, tear over the fresh basil and parsley leaves and stir through. Remove the pan from the heat.

Finely slice the courgette lengthways into approximately 1mm slices and dice the Brie into small pieces.

Spoon the rice-and-tomato-and-onion mixture into two small greased ovenproof dishes, ramekins or bowls. Scatter the Brie on top. Then lay the courgette slices over the cheese so that they overlap, and brush or drizzle with a little oil.

Cook in the preheated oven for 15 minutes until lightly toasted on top. Remove from the oven, allow to cool slightly, then serve.

TIPS: If, like me, you are a big cheese fiend, add grated Parmesan or another hard strong cheese on top of the courgette slices before popping into the oven.

To make it extra special, add chopped pieces of bacon to the mixture. Fry the bacon first in the sauté pan, then add the onion and rice and follow the main recipe from there.

SORT-OF PAELLA

The star of the show in this paella is the simple coloured rice, cooked al dente, accentuated with bright red tomatoes and little green peas. This recipe is delicious on its own, or can be used as a base. Feel free to add chopped peppers, seasonal vegetables, any meat or fish of your choice, a glass of white wine, a splash of sherry – whatever your budget or your cupboard will allow. But for me, nothing beats a fistful of tiny little prawns, half a cup of peas and a spoon to eat it with.

Traditional paella uses saffron strands to colour the rice, but I use bright yellow turmeric powder instead. This is a fraction of the cost and much more versatile, as it can be used in Saag Aloo (see page 137), Simple Spiced Potato Soup (see page 54), and many, many curry recipes besides. Traditional paella also uses a fat short-grain rice, but I use the ordinary long-grain store cupboard stuff because it's what I have to hand. And a rice is a rice is a rice, as far as I'm concerned.

Serves 2

2 tablespoons oil

1 onion

2 cloves of garlic

500ml chicken stock

1 scant teaspoon turmeric powder

4 tablespoons tinned chopped tomatoes or 2 large ripe tomatoes, chopped

150g rice

2 sprigs of fresh thyme

70g fresh or frozen peas, or green beans, cut into lengths

150g fresh or frozen cooked prawns

Heat the oil in a medium frying pan or sauté pan. Peel and finely slice the onion, peel and finely chop or crush the garlic, and put both into the pan to soften for a few minutes on a medium heat. Take care not to brown them, as the slightly burnt taste will permeate through the whole dish.

Meanwhile bring the chicken stock to a simmer in a separate small saucepan and shake in the turmeric.

Add the chopped tomatoes and the rice to the frying pan with the onion and garlic and stir. Chop the thyme, add to the pan and stir again briefly to combine. Pour a cup of the hot stock into the pan, then stir well to stop the rice from sticking.

When the stock has been absorbed by the rice, add another cup. Repeat until all the stock is used up, or the rice is soft. Unlike risotto, you do not need to stir paella constantly, but a little stir every now and again is helpful to stop the rice from sticking to the pan.

When the rice is almost cooked, add the frozen peas or beans and the cooked prawns, stir and cook for 5 minutes, until the vegetables are tender and the prawns are warmed through. Remove from the heat and leave to stand for a few minutes before serving, to allow the flavours to settle.

VEGETABLE DISHES

The great thing about vegetables is that there are no hard and fast rules, so you can use whatever you have to hand in most cases. Go on, be a bit daring. You can't go far wrong. Try using the following list as a 'swapping' guide.

Roots: potatoes, carrots, parsnips, turnips, swede, sweet potatoes

Oniony things: onions (red or white), garlic, leeks

Greens: broccoli, peas, green beans, runner beans

Leaves: spinach, cabbage, spring greens, kale, even lettuce (but finely chop it and throw into the pan for just the last 30 seconds)

Frozen veg is extremely handy and is usually much cheaper than its fresh counterparts. I keep frozen green beans and spinach on standby most of the time to toss into dinners or as a side dish. Tinned carrots and potatoes are very useful to have in the store cupboard too.

And if all else fails, sling all your veg into a pot together and make them into a curry, such as the Vegetable Masala Curry (see page 119).

GNOCCHI

Gnocchi are a cross between a dumpling and a sort of potato pasta – comforting, thick and soft. They are easy to 'gnocch' together from a tin of potatoes, or boil fresh potatoes if you prefer. Traditionally served with butter and herbs, I toss mine in home-made pesto (see Best-o Pesto on page 84) or top with Use-Me-For-Anything Tomato Sauce (see page 83).

Serves 4

500g tinned potatoes (drained weight)

a handful of fresh parsley

1 egg, beaten

100g flour, plus extra to knead the dough

Place the potatoes in a large saucepan, cover with water and bring to the boil. Reduce to a simmer and cook to warm through – around 5 minutes. While they are boiling, finely chop the parsley.

When the potatoes are done, lift them out with a slotted spoon and pop into a mixing bowl, reserving the water to use in a minute. Mash the potatoes quickly, stir in the egg and parsley, and mix well to combine. Add the flour and work into the mashed potato to form a thick, floury mixture.

Tip the mixture out on to a floured surface and use your hands to work it for a few minutes to create a soft dough.

Take a handful of the dough and roll it into a long thin sausage, about 2.5cm thick. Cut this sausage into pieces, also about 2.5cm long. Press a fork into the top of each piece to create the ridges and place the finished gnocchi on the side. Repeat with the rest of the dough.

Bring the pan of water back to the boil. Lower the gnocchi in a few at a time and remove with a slotted spoon when they rise to the surface. Repeat until all the gnocchi have been cooked.

TIPS: Substitute sweet potatoes for the normal tinned potatoes (the sweet potatoes will need peeling, cutting into cubes and boiling to cook through, since they're not tinned) and add a pinch of dried chilli flakes and a peeled and crushed clove of garlic instead of the parsley.

For amazing parsnip and thyme gnocchi, use 250g parsnips (boil to cook through first), instead of half the potatoes and fresh thyme leaves in place of the parsley.

Leftover gnocchi can be frozen in an airtight container, and defrosted by bringing to the boil in a saucepan of water and cooking through. Alternatively, defrost at room temperature, pop into a roasting dish with a little oil, and roast for 20 minutes at 180°C/350°F/gas 4 for a cross between a roast potato and a potato croquette.

COURGETTE AND MINT FRITTERS

The humble courgette – you either love it or you hate it! However, courgettes are cheap and abundant in the summer months, and extremely versatile. These fritters are great as a standalone snack with home-made raita dip (see below) or served with sausages and ketchup.

Makes 4 chunky or 6 thin fritters

1 courgette

a handful of fresh mint

a handful of fresh coriander

a handful of fresh parsley

1 egg, beaten

1–2 heaped tablespoons plain flour

2 tablespoons oil

50g natural yoghurt

Finely grate the courgette into a large mixing bowl. Chop the herbs and add about three-quarters to the courgette in the bowl. Set the rest aside for the yoghurt dip.

Mix the beaten egg into the courgette and herbs with a fork. Add 1 tablespoon of the flour and continue to mix until it has formed a batter. You may need to add a little more flour to make the batter thicker than a pancake mixture. Ideally it will stick to the prongs of the fork but come loose with a shake.

Heat the oil in a frying pan and dollop a pretty level tablespoon of batter in. Flatten with the back of the spoon and shape the edges to form a rough circle. Repeat until you run out of space in the pan, with a little gap around each for ease of turning. You may have to cook the fritters in batches. Fry on a low heat for a few minutes, until golden and crispy on the underside. Using a spatula, turn over and cook on the other side. Repeat until all batter is used up.

Stir the remaining herbs into the natural yoghurt and serve with the fritters.

TIP: Add cheese to make these extra special – for the recipe above 50g of Cheddar or another hard, strong cheese, or a Greek cheese like feta, would complement the flavours perfectly.

BUBBLES AND SQUEAKS

Traditionally a Monday mash-up of the Sunday roast, a comforting, easy bubble and squeak is something I have been making for years. It's one of the first things I taught myself to cook and is still a firm favourite. If you don't have a leftover Sunday roast lying about, here's how to make it from scratch. I eat mine with a fried egg and some ketchup, but depending on your budget and preferences, you can serve bubble and squeak with sausages, or chicken and veg, or on its own as a lunch or snack.

Makes 8 patties (2 per person)

1 vegetable stock cube, dissolved in 500ml boiling water

2 potatoes

1 carrot

2 tablespoons oil, plus extra to fry the patties

1 onion, peeled

¼ of a cabbage

1 egg, beaten

1 tablespoon flour

Bring the vegetable stock to the boil in a medium-sized saucepan.

Wash then dice the potatoes and carrot (I don't peel mine, but this is optional) and add to the stock.

While the root veg are cooking, take a separate frying pan or non-stick saucepan and put the oil into it. Finely slice the onion and cabbage and add to the saucepan. Fry gently until the onion is soft, stirring occasionally to allow it all to cook.

When the root veg are cooked, drain and tip back into the saucepan. Add the onions and cabbage and mash together thoroughly with a masher. Add the egg and flour and stir through.

This is an optional stage but it helps the mixture hold together more successfully – however, if you're in a rush and willing to keep an eye on the patties when frying them, it's not essential. Scoop the mash mixture into a bowl and refrigerate it for 1 to 2 hours to allow it to set a little.

Heat some oil in a frying pan and dollop a heaped tablespoon of mashed veg mixture into it. Flatten slightly with the back of a fork or spatula and cook on a medium heat until golden and crisp on one side (it depends on your hob, but mine takes about 7 minutes). Turn the patty over and cook the other side. You may need to fry them in batches.

TIPS: You can use pretty much any vegetables you like in bubble and squeak. I like to make a posh version with parsnip and red onion every now and again. Sweet potato is also a good base, extra carrot will make them sweeter and peas will sneak some extra green veg into your kids. Play with the mixture and see what you come up with.

You might want to add a little grated hard strong cheese to the mix, if you like that sort of thing.

The cooked patties keep in the fridge for a few days, so you could have them another day with bacon and an egg as brunch, too. Or you could be a heathen, like me, and snack on them straight from the fridge.

You can keep the enriched stock from cooking the root vegetables to use in another dish – cool and store in an airtight container in the fridge for 3 days or in the freezer for up to 3 months.

VEGETABLE MASALA CURRY

The trick with curry – good curry – is to allow it to cook slowly and gently in order that the flavours infuse and meld together in an amalgamation of spicy goodness. I let mine simmer gently for about 40 minutes, checking and adding extra liquid if it starts to dry out. However, once the vegetables are cooked through you can take the pan off the heat and leave it to cool for the same flavour-infusing effect without using so much gas or electricity.

Serves 4

1 onion

1 clove of garlic

1 small red chilli or a pinch of the dried stuff

a splash of oil

1 heaped teaspoon ground cumin

2 potatoes or 500g tinned potatoes (drained weight)

2 carrots or 200g tinned carrots (drained weight)

a fistful of fresh parsley

a fistful of fresh coriander

200ml vegetable stock, plus extra if needed

100g green beans or 60g fresh spinach

1 x 400g carton or tin of chopped tomatoes

250ml natural yoghurt

Peel and chop the onion and garlic, finely slice the chilli, and place in a large sauté pan on a low heat with the oil. Add the cumin (and dried chilli, if using) and cook until softened.

Wash and chop (or drain if using tinned vegetables) the potatoes and carrots, and add to the pot. Chop the herbs and throw into the pan. Pour in the stock, add the green beans or spinach and the chopped tomatoes and leave to simmer on a low heat.

Simmer gently for 40 minutes, checking and adding a little more stock or water if it starts to dry out. Alternatively, to use less gas or electricity, once the vegetables are cooked through take the pan off the heat and leave to stand for the same 40 minutes, and just put it back on the heat for a blast to warm through at the end.

Stir in the yoghurt before serving.

TIPS: Allow to cool, then freeze leftovers, or stuff into pitta breads for next day's lunch.

Turn this into a vegetable korma by using coconut yoghurt instead of natural yoghurt – which is far less costly than the more usual coconut milk! – and replace the cumin with turmeric.

NOT MEATBALLS

These 'not meatballs' are adapted from a recipe in the *Abel & Cole Veg Box Companion* cookbook. They are a great veggie alternative to meatballs and a favourite in my household. Delicious served with spaghetti and tomato sauce – or simply a carton of chopped tomatoes heated through would be a perfect accompaniment.

Serves 2

1 aubergine

1 red or white onion

1 fat clove of garlic

1 red chilli

1 tablespoon finely chopped black olives

3 tablespoons oil

zest and juice of 1 lemon or 2 tablespoons bottled lemon juice, plus extra to serve

1 slice of bread, fresh or slightly stale (this is a good way to use up old bread)

a handful of fresh basil, plus extra to serve

Cut the stems off the ends of the aubergines and halve lengthways. Dice the flesh into chunks and pop into a medium non-stick saucepan or frying pan. Peel and finely slice the onion and garlic, chop the chilli as finely as you can, and add these plus the olives to the aubergine in the pan with 1 tablespoon of the oil. Cook on a medium heat for about 10 minutes to brown and soften.

Grate over the lemon zest, squeeze in the lemon juice and, once the aubergines are soft, tip everything into a mixing bowl. Grate the bread over the top, finely chop the basil and mix in well.

Shape the mixture into tablespoon-sized balls with your hands. Put the remaining 2 tablespoons of oil in a frying pan and carefully fry the aubergine balls in batches until browned all over. Remove with a slotted spoon and serve with extra lemon juice and torn basil to taste.

BABA GHANOUSH

Baba ghanoush is a popular Middle Eastern dish, often served as a dip with pitta breads. I sometimes add cooked chickpeas to mine for a simple, flavoursome curry, or toss it through pasta with fresh mint for an easy lunch. I highly recommend cooking the aubergines over an open flame for a deep, smoky intensity – I hold mine over a medium gas hob with a pair of barbecue tongs and my sleeves rolled up – although charring under the grill is nearly as good. For the accompanying toasted pittas, slice pitta breads through the middle then cut into triangles, brush with a little oil and pop under the grill for 4 to 5 minutes until crispy.

Serves 2

1 large aubergine

1 fat clove of garlic

1 tablespoon oil

a pinch of ground cumin

juice and zest of ½ a lemon or 1 tablespoon bottled lemon juice

1 x 400g carton or tin of chopped tomatoes

a handful of fresh coriander

Chop the stem off the end of the aubergine and pierce the skin all over with a fork or sharp knife. Cook under a hot grill or over a low open flame for 10 minutes, turning to char the skin on all sides for a deep smoky intensity.

Cut the aubergine in half and remove the seeds, scooping them out with a teaspoon and discarding. Then spoon the flesh from the skin (which you also discard) into a small non-stick saucepan or frying pan.

Peel and crush the garlic, or chop very finely, and add to the aubergine along with the oil and cumin. Soften on a low heat for a few minutes, then add the lemon zest and juice and the chopped tomatoes. Stir and cook until heated through. Finely chop the coriander and stir through just before serving.

TIP: Add cooked red or brown lentils to leftovers to make a thick, spicy pasta sauce.

MUSHROOM CHASSEUR

This simple, delicious mushroom casserole is perfect easy comfort for cold evenings, served with a heap of fluffy mashed potatoes, or atop some plain rice for a delicious dinner.

Serves 2

1 onion

2 fat cloves of garlic

400g mushrooms

2 tablespoons oil

a fistful of fresh thyme or a shake of mixed dried herbs

100ml red wine

1 x 400g carton or tin of chopped tomatoes

1 vegetable stock cube

Peel and finely chop the onion and garlic. Gently clean any excess earth from the mushrooms with a clean tea towel and break them up. Pour the oil into a sauté pan or frying pan, or a large lidded casserole dish, and add the prepared vegetables. Chop the thyme and scatter on top, and cook for 5 to 10 minutes on a low heat until the onions are softening.

Pour in the wine, stir in the chopped tomatoes and crumble in the stock cube, then bring to a bubbling boil for 5 minutes. Reduce the heat, cover and simmer for 1 hour. Alternatively, to use less energy when cooking, blast on a high heat for 10 minutes, stirring constantly to prevent burning and sticking, then remove from the heat, cover and leave to stand for 1 hour – which will meld the flavours together and thicken the sauce without using so much gas or electricity. Simply heat through on a medium heat to serve.

TIPS: Stir ½ a teaspoon of mustard into mashed potatoes for a fantastic pairing.

This dish makes a gorgeous pasta sauce for next day's lunch or dinner, or can be frozen in an airtight container for up to 3 months. Serve any leftovers on top of couscous for a great hot or cold snack.

KERALAN AUBERGINE CURRY

One of my favourite restaurants in Southend specializes in Keralan cuisine – and when I couldn't afford to go out for it but really wanted a rich, spicy curry, I decided to make my own version. Aubergines are comparatively expensive to buy on their own, so I normally buy a bag of three or four, and eat aubergines all week. Check out the index for more ideas of what to cook with aubergines. Serve this dish with plain or lemon rice.

Serves 2

2 aubergines

a pinch of salt

1 onion

1 fat clove of garlic

2 tablespoons oil

2 red chillies or 2 pinches of dried chilli flakes

½ teaspoon turmeric

½ teaspoon ground cumin

¼ teaspoon English mustard

zest and juice of ½ a lemon or 1 tablespoon bottled lemon juice

1 x 400g carton or tin of chopped tomatoes

a handful of coriander, to serve

natural yoghurt, to serve

Cut the stems from the ends of the aubergines, and pierce the skin all over with a fork or sharp knife. Pop into a mixing bowl or saucepan and cover with cold water and a pinch of salt to reduce the natural bitter flavour. Leave to stand for 20 minutes.

Meanwhile, peel and finely chop the onion and garlic, and toss into a medium frying pan or non-stick saucepan with the oil. Sweat the onions on a very low heat, stirring to make sure they don't burn or stick. Finely chop the chillies and add to the pan, along with the turmeric, cumin and mustard. Stir and cook the spices a little.

Remove the aubergines from the water, cut into chunks and add to the pan. Stir in well to coat with the now-spicy oil, add the lemon juice and zest, if using, and turn up the heat to medium to brown the edges of the aubergine chunks. Pour over the chopped tomatoes and simmer for 10 minutes, until the aubergines are tender.

Finely chop the coriander. Serve the curry with a dollop of natural yoghurt and a scattering of chopped coriander on top.

TIP: If you have a spare aubergine, use it to make Melitzanosalata. Prepare the aubergine as above, but instead fry the chunks until golden in 2 tablespoons of oil with 1 peeled and finely chopped or crushed clove of garlic. Remove from the heat, and stir in the zest and juice of ½ a lemon or 1 tablespoon bottled lemon juice and 50g feta cheese or other Greek-style goat's cheese. Mash together with a fork to combine and serve as a dip with bread or tossed with pasta.

CHESTNUT AND RED WINE CASSEROLE

I first made this after Christmas, when the chestnuts that are usually pricey and stacked high in supermarkets for the festive season are suddenly reduced to pennies as they seek to clear their stock. Chestnuts have a pleasantly meaty texture and 'bite' to them, so although this is a vegan dish, it satisfies most of my carnivorous friends. It's not as cheffy and pretentious as it sounds – it can be thrown together in a pan with little effort, and is great with a pile of fluffy mash (stir in ½ a teaspoon of mustard for absolute perfection!) and cooked cabbage or other green vegetables.

Serves 2

1 onion

2 cloves of garlic

2 large carrots or parsnips

a splash of oil

a fistful of fresh thyme

200ml red wine

1 teaspoon Marmite or Vegemite

1 vegetable stock cube, dissolved in 300ml boiling water

1 x 400g carton or tin of chopped tomatoes

100g mushrooms

200g pre-cooked, vacuum-packed chestnuts

a squeeze of lemon juice

Peel and finely slice the onion and garlic, wash and dice the carrots or parsnips, and place them all in a medium frying pan or sauté pan along with the oil. Chop the thyme and scatter on top, and cook on a medium heat until the onions and carrots start to soften.

Add the wine, Marmite or Vegemite and stock, bring to a vigorous boil, then turn down the heat. Pour in the chopped tomatoes, and simmer gently. Gently clean any excess earth from the mushrooms with a clean tea towel, then break them up and add to the pan along with the chestnuts.

Turn the heat down low and cook for 40 minutes with the lid off, stirring occasionally. If you don't want to use all of that energy cooking for so long, bring the heat right up to blast it through for 5 minutes, then remove from the heat, cover with a lid and leave to stand for half an hour. Heat through again slowly – the sitting time will have allowed the flavours to meld and deepen and the sauce to thicken beautifully, without costing so much in gas or electricity.

Serve with a little lemon juice squeezed over.

TIPS: Tinned carrots and mushrooms work just as well in this recipe in place of fresh ones – making it something that can be thrown together from a well-stocked store cupboard.

This will keep in the fridge for 2 to 3 days if allowed to cool and stored in an airtight container, or in the freezer for up to 3 months.

MOROCCAN NOT-A-TAGINE

This tagine uses my three staple spices – turmeric, cumin and paprika – to deliver a gorgeous sweet and spicy dinner. I made it for Xanthe Clay from the *Daily Telegraph* when she visited for an article called 'My 49p lunch with a girl called Jack'. In her words 'the food is very fine, and it's also healthy' – so what are you waiting for? Serve with couscous or rice and optional green vegetables.

Serves 4

1 large onion

2 cloves of garlic

1 red chilli

a splash of oil

zest and juice of 1 lemon
or 1 tablespoon of bottled
lemon juice

1 heaped teaspoon turmeric

1 heaped teaspoon
ground cumin

1 heaped teaspoon paprika

1 x 400g carton or tin
of chopped tomatoes

1 tablespoon honey or sugar

a handful of fresh mint, chopped

a handful of fresh coriander,
chopped

2 large potatoes or 500g tinned
potatoes (drained weight)

2 large carrots or 400g tinned
carrots (drained weight)

50g prunes

1 beef stock cube, dissolved
in 500ml boiling water

Peel and dice the onion, peel and crush the garlic and chop the chilli, and place in a sauté pan with the oil, lemon zest, turmeric, cumin and paprika. Cook gently over a low heat until soft. Then add the lemon juice, chopped tomatoes, honey or sugar, mint and coriander, and stir everything together.

Chop the potatoes and carrots and add to the pan, along with the prunes. Pour in enough beef stock to cover – usually around 500ml. Leave the pan simmering, covered, on the hob for 30 minutes, but you will need to check it every now and again to ensure that it is not drying out. If that's the case, add more stock or water.

The stew is ready when the vegetables are tender but not mushy, and the sauce thick but not clumpy.

MUSHROOM STROGANOFF

I like to make my stroganoff with plenty of sauce, especially when serving with a pile of fluffy rice – then it turns into ideal comforting 'bowl food'. Add the yoghurt just before serving to stop it splitting. The quantities given here are easily doubled to make a delicious meal for friends or family.

Serves 2

150ml yoghurt

juice of ½ a lemon or 2 teaspoons bottled lemon juice

1 small onion

250g mushrooms

1 tablespoon oil

a scant ½ teaspoon English mustard

1 teaspoon paprika

100ml vegetable stock

First, tip the yoghurt into a small bowl, add the lemon juice and let it stand for 5 minutes. This will sour the yoghurt.

Peel and finely slice the onion, then clean the mushrooms and break them up. Put both into a sauté pan or frying pan on a low heat with the oil. Add the mustard and paprika, and stir into the mixture. Cook on a low heat for 10 minutes to soften the onions and start to brown the mushrooms.

Pour in the stock and turn the heat up to medium, stirring to mix. Allow to simmer on a medium heat for 10 minutes.

Before serving, remove from the heat and stir the yoghurt through.

POTATO SALAD WITH GREEK CHEESE, COURGETTE AND YOGHURT

Like many of my recipes, this was a toss-together of some 'fridge stuff' – some rogue Greek cheese and a courgette that was kicking about. Harking back to my Cypriot roots for what was initially going to be a tzatziki, this ended up as something else entirely. The sauce or dip, or whatever it should be called, is immensely versatile, but my favourite thing to do with it is toss it with pre-boiled tinned potatoes as in the recipe here. These quantities are easily halved for smaller households, or doubled for parties and potato fiends.

Serves 4 as a snack or
2 as a main meal

1 courgette

a fistful of fresh mint

a fistful of fresh parsley

1 clove of garlic or ½ an onion

1 tablespoon oil

zest and juice of 1 lemon or 2 tablespoons bottled lemon juice

50g Greek cheese
(feta-style or goat's cheese)

120ml natural yoghurt

500g tinned potatoes
(drained weight)

Preheat the oven to 180°C/350°F/gas 4.

Chop the stalk and the bottom from the courgette. Dice and tip into a shallow roasting dish.

Pop the mint and parsley into a tea cup and chop finely with kitchen scissors. Peel the garlic or onion. Pour the oil over the herbs, add the grated lemon zest, squeeze the lemon juice in and press the garlic in, if using. If you don't have any garlic, then very finely chop the onion and add it to the dressing.

Stir well and pour over the courgette pieces, shaking to coat them in the dressing. Pop into the preheated oven for 20 to 30 minutes to roast.

When the courgette is cooked, tip into a bowl, pouring in all of the juices from the roasting dish. Crumble over the cheese and mash roughly with a fork. Add the yoghurt and mix well. Drain the potatoes and toss through the sauce until coated, then serve.

TIPS: If you are short of time or don't want to use the energy heating the oven, simply grate the courgette and mix with the rest of the dressing ingredients. The flavour will be less intense but still utterly delicious.

This dish is very similar to the Creamy Greek Cheese and Courgette Pasta (see page 98), so why not roast your courgettes at the same time and make both.

PANZANELLA

Panzanella sounds a lot more fancy than it is – simply a bowl of stale bread and mushy tomatoes! I finish off any leftover soda bread in this recipe, but the two 'heels' of a normal loaf are a good substitute. If you don't have any mushy tomatoes in the bottom of the fridge, drain a carton of chopped tomatoes and use that instead.

Serves 2

a generous handful of fresh basil

a generous handful of fresh parsley

4 tablespoons oil

zest and juice of ½ a lemon or 1 tablespoon bottled lemon juice

1–2 thick slices of leftover bread

4 overripe tomatoes or 1 x 400g carton or tin of chopped tomatoes, drained

2 tablespoons sliced black olives

First, make the dressing for the salad. Finely chop half of the basil and parsley into a small bowl or jug, leaving half as whole leaves to toss through the salad. Add the oil, lemon juice and zest, if using, and mix well.

Tear or cut the bread into chunks, and place in a bowl, then pour the dressing over the top. Roughly chop the tomatoes and mix with the bread, then add the sliced olives. Stir in the remaining basil and parsley leaves.

The salad can be eaten immediately, but is also delicious refrigerated for an hour or so to allow the bread to soften and soak up the flavours.

COLCANNON

Colcannon is a traditional Irish recipe made with kale, spring greens or cabbage – depending on what you have available. Colcannon was a staple of my childhood but my mother, born and raised in Belfast, called it 'champ'. We used to eat it with a pile of sausages and gravy, and always had seconds. When cooking potatoes in a dish like this, I leave the skins on for texture, extra fibre and goodness, and admittedly laziness – but it's a personal choice. I also don't mash until everything's smooth because I like my Irish grub rough and chunky. Serve with sausages or chicken, or eat as it is straight from the pot. The quantities are easily doubled.

Serves 2 as a side dish

500g potatoes (fresh or tinned)

2 large handfuls of cabbage, spring greens or curly kale

1 large onion

a knob of butter, or more to taste

If using fresh potatoes, wash and dice them. If using tinned potatoes, drain and leave them whole. Bring a saucepan of water to the boil, pop the potatoes in and simmer until tender – 20 minutes for fresh potatoes, 5 minutes for tinned ones.

Finely chop the cabbage, greens or kale and peel and finely chop the onion. When the potatoes are soft, toss the cabbage and onion into the saucepan to blanch for just a minute or two.

Drain the vegetables and tip back into the saucepan. Add the butter and mash until it has a rough texture – or continue to mash and add more butter until smoother.

TIPS: Make leftovers into colcannon gnocchi – just use in place of the potatoes in the Gnocchi recipe (see page 115).

Leftovers can also be turned into potato cakes. Mix in 1–2 tablespoons of flour (depending on how much colcannon you have), shape into patties and fry in a little oil on a medium heat for a few minutes each side until golden.

SAAG ALOO

Saag aloo means spiced spinach potatoes. You can use fresh or frozen spinach in this dish – just grab whatever you find you have. For frozen spinach, either run it under warm water to defrost, leave in a dish at room temperature or defrost gently in the microwave. You need to drain the excess water and then it's ready to use. These deliciously spicy potatoes make a pleasant lunch dish for 1 or a side dish for 2, served with something like the Keralan Aubergine Curry (see page 126).

Serves 1–2

70g chopped spinach leaves or defrosted and drained frozen spinach

3 tablespoons oil

a scant teaspoon English or wholegrain mustard

a scant teaspoon ground cumin or turmeric (whichever is to hand)

1 x 500g tin of tinned potatoes, drained

Preheat the oven to 180°C/350°F/gas 4.

Place the spinach in a mixing bowl. Add the oil, mustard and cumin or turmeric to the bowl and mix well to combine. Chop the potatoes into small cubes and add to the spiced spinach mixture. Mix again to coat the potatoes evenly.

Tip out into a non-stick roasting dish and cook in the preheated oven for 20 minutes, turning occasionally to prevent sticking and to cook evenly.

TIPS: If there are any leftovers, stir in 1 tablespoon natural yoghurt and ½ a very finely chopped onion to make a potato salad that is delicious cold for next day's lunch.

Substitute chickpeas for the potatoes. Toss the chickpeas into the roasting dish with the spinach, oil and spices and cook in the preheated oven for 15 minutes.

FISHES

Did you know that pilchards are adult sardines? Most sardines and pilchards sold in the UK are preserved in tins, not sold as fresh fish, which make them an ideal standby to have in the store cupboard. I buy tinned sardines in oil and drain them, reserving the oil to cook Sicilian-style Sardines with Pasta and Green Beans (see page 152). Or I keep the oil in the fridge to use as a marinade for a fish recipe later in the week, or I mix it into chopped tomatoes with fresh basil leaves and a splash of lemon juice to make a quick and easy pasta sauce with rich, Mediterranean flavours.

While experimenting with tinned fish, I came across herring roes, a strong but meltingly soft fish that makes it ideal for suppers like Scampi Roes (see page 150). However, my most surprising discovery was a jar of fish paste – a staple of childhood sandwiches, but now the secret ingredient in Creamy Salmon Pasta with a Chilli Lemon Kick (see page 144). One of my blog readers swears that it tastes like an expensive salmon dinner at a certain chain of Italian restaurants!

In the supermarket, I buy bulk bags of assorted white frozen fish fillets, tins of sardines and herring roes, and jars of fish paste and anchovies. The fresh fish counter is a rare treat – but I must confess to the occasional packet of salmon trimmings when I want to make a smart lunch.

JACK'S SIMPLE FISH PIE

I love a fish pie but, when time is tight, I make fish in a white sauce and serve it with a pile of fluffy mash with cheese instead. Fancy restaurants would call that 'deconstructed' – I call it 'quicker and easier'. This recipe below is a delicious midweek treat.

Serves 4–6

1kg potatoes, fresh or tinned

1 large onion

a handful of chopped
fresh thyme

350g skinless firm white fish

350g skinless smoked haddock

300ml whole milk, plus
extra to mash the potatoes

4 eggs

30g butter, plus extra to
mash the potatoes

50g hard strong cheese

a handful of fresh parsley,
chopped

2 heaped tablespoons plain flour

70g spinach leaves

Preheat the oven to 180°C/350°F/gas 4.

Wash and dice the potatoes (or drain if using tinned ones) and bring to the boil in a large saucepan of water. Reduce to a medium heat and cook until tender – 20 minutes for fresh potatoes, 5 minutes for tinned.

Meanwhile, poach the fish. Peel and slice the onion and put into a large sauté pan or saucepan with the thyme. Add the fish, cover with the milk, and poach on a low heat for around 8 minutes. Remove the pan from the heat, take out the fish and onion pieces and place on a plate. Flake the fish with a fork. Reserve the poaching liquid to make the sauce with later.

Boil or poach the eggs in a small saucepan for 6 minutes. Drain and carefully spoon poached eggs on to the fish plate, or leave boiled eggs to cool and then peel. Check the potatoes – when cooked, drain and tip back into the saucepan. Mash with a little milk and butter. Grate the cheese into the mash and stir well to melt through. Stir in the chopped parsley.

Melt the butter in a pan over a low heat and add 1 tablespoon of the flour. Stir well with a wooden spoon to make a thick paste. Add the other tablespoon of flour and repeat. Now take a tablespoon of the poaching liquid and stir it into the paste. Repeat, gradually adding more liquid, until blended together in a thick sauce. You may not need to use all the poaching liquid. Add the spinach, stir to wilt, then tip in the cooked eggs, mashing them with the back of a fork to break up. Add the onion, then the flaked fish, and mix everything together well.

Spoon into a large ovenproof casserole dish and top with the mash, starting at the edge of the dish and working inwards, using a fork to fluff up the top. Bake for 20 minutes, until the mash is golden and crispy on top.

TIPS: Instead of one big pie, make individual pies to freeze separately. Fill small freezer and ovenproof dishes half full with the fish mixture, then top with the mash. Do not cook but instead allow to cool, cover and freeze for up to 3 months. To cook, bake straight from frozen in an oven preheated to 180°C/350°F/gas 4 for 30 minutes. Or, for speed, store the small pies in Tupperware and cook in the microwave.

FISHY CAKES

I usually make these in miniature, so where the recipe below will typically yield 8 chunky fish cakes, I make around 30 fish nuggets – perfect for small children to dip into 'red sauce'. If using tinned pilchards in tomato sauce, reserve as much of the sauce as you can, squidge a bit of tomato purée in to thicken, add a dash of vinegar and a dash of lemon. Voila – home-made ketchup!

Makes 8 fish cakes

500g tinned potatoes, drained

500g tinned pilchards, drained

a generous fistful of fresh parsley

2 slices bread (this is a good way to use up bread past its best)

1 tablespoon flour, plus extra to dust your hands

1 egg

2 tablespoons oil

First, bring the potatoes to the boil in a saucepan of water, and then reduce to a medium heat. Cook for about 5 minutes until very soft. Test by prodding them with a fork – if they yield easily, they're good to go. Drain the potatoes, tip into a mixing bowl and mash with a masher or a fork until almost smooth.

Add the pilchards to the bowl, working them into the mash with a fork to break up and combine them. Pilchards have soft bones, but sometimes the harder spines won't break as easily. Be vigilant and pick out anything that won't mash in.

Chop the parsley, add it to the mash-and-fish mixture and mix well. Chill the mixture for half an hour in the fridge. This is important, as it helps keep the patties together while cooking!

When the mixture is chilled, remove from the fridge and divide into 8 evenly sized balls. Grate the bread on to a plate, or blitz in a blender to make breadcrumbs, and stir in the flour. In a separate bowl, beat the egg.

Get a frying or sauté pan ready with the oil in the bottom on a medium heat. Take one of the patties with floured hands, dip it in the beaten egg and dip each side in the breadcrumbs, then carefully pop it in the frying pan. Repeat until you've filled the pan. Fry each patty for 5 minutes before carefully turning over with a spatula to cook for 5 minutes on the other side. You will probably need to cook them in batches – unless you have an extremely big pan!

TIPS: You can use almost any tinned fish to make these fish cakes – but I always have a tin of pilchards and a tin of potatoes on standby.

For healthier fish cakes, bake them in a preheated oven at 180°C/350°F/gas 4 for 15 to 20 minutes, until golden and crispy.

You can halve the quantities to make 4 fish cakes or freeze any leftovers. Simply reheat in a low oven to defrost. They are also delicious the next day, cut into strips and served in a roll, as a grown-up gourmet version of fish-finger sandwiches.

SIMPLE PRAWNS WITH FETA AND TOMATOES

This Mediterranean-inspired dish is one of those midweek specials, taking just minutes to cook, but still delicious. For winter comfort, add a chopped red chilli and spoon over fluffy rice; for a summer twist, toss with pasta.

Serves 2

1 tablespoon oil

1 onion

1 clove of garlic

1 x 400g carton or tin of chopped tomatoes

170g cooked peeled prawns

a handful of fresh parsley

50g Greek cheese (such as feta)

Put the oil into a medium frying pan or sauté pan. Peel and finely dice the onion, peel and crush or finely slice the garlic, and add to the pan. Cook on a gentle heat for a few minutes until the onion starts to soften.

Pour over the chopped tomatoes and stir thoroughly to mix with the oil, garlic and onion. Toss in the prawns and turn the heat up to medium to warm through.

Chop the parsley and crumble the cheese. Serve the tomatoey prawns with the cheese and herbs scattered on top.

TIPS: To make a dish with a kick – a sort of simple prawn jalfrezi – leave out the cheese and add 1 chopped red chilli, 1 sliced pepper and the juice of ½ a lemon or lime to the pan at the same time as the onions and garlic.

For a sweeter summery version, replace the parsley with fresh basil and add a splash of orange juice or grated orange zest with the chopped tomatoes.

CREAMY SALMON PASTA WITH A CHILLI LEMON KICK

This speedy fish supper – really simply a tinkering with a cheap jar of fish paste – takes just a few lazy minutes to put together and tastes absolutely divine. The sharpness of the lemon complements the salmon flavour and the yoghurt lends a creamy subtlety. When I first put this recipe on my blog, over 100 people tried it, admitting disbelief that such simple ingredients could make such a yummy meal.

Serves 2

160g pasta

1 onion

1 small red chilli

a bunch of flat-leaf parsley, plus extra to serve

1 tablespoon oil

zest and juice of ½ a lemon or 1 tablespoon bottled lemon juice, plus extra to serve

150ml natural yoghurt

1 x 75g jar of salmon (or other fish) paste

Bring a medium saucepan of water to the boil, and add the pasta. Reduce to a simmer and allow to cook for 8 to 10 minutes (or according to the packet instructions).

Meanwhile, peel and finely slice the onion, and very finely chop the chilli and parsley. Put into a frying pan with the oil, lemon zest and juice and cook over a medium heat to soften the onion.

When the pasta is cooked, remove from the heat and drain.

Quickly stir the yoghurt and fish paste into the onions to warm through. Tip the pasta into the pan and stir to coat with the sauce. Serve, garnishing with extra chopped parsley and lemon juice if desired.

EASY SALMON PASTA

This quick and simple pasta dish can be enjoyed hot or cold, and is a great use for the bags of smoked salmon trimmings that you can find at most local supermarkets – or, if you have a local fishmonger, it's worth asking them.

Serves 2

200g pasta

1 tablespoon oil

1 onion

zest and juice of 1 lemon or 2 tablespoons bottled lemon juice

150g smoked salmon trimmings

a handful of fresh parsley

Bring a saucepan of water to the boil. Put in the pasta and cook according to the packet instructions, usually around 8 to 10 minutes.

While the pasta is cooking, put the oil into a small frying or sauté pan. Peel and finely slice the onion and add to the pan, then grate in the lemon zest. Squeeze over the lemon juice, and cook on a low heat until the onion is softened.

When the pasta is done, remove from the heat and drain. Tip the salmon trimmings into the pan with the onion and stir through quickly until opaque. Add the pasta to the pan, stir to combine with the salmon, onions and lemony oil, and dish up into bowls. Finely chop the parsley and sprinkle over to serve.

TIPS: If you like your pasta to come with a sauce, add 2 tablespoons natural yoghurt to the onions as they cook.

For a real budget version, replace the salmon trimmings with a few crab sticks, cut into chunks.

SPAGHETTI WITH COCKLES

Cockles are a speciality where I live – a few miles to the east of Leigh-on-Sea, a small traditional fishing village set on the Thames Estuary. Early summer memories are defined by walking into Leigh with my parents, and walking home again with a paper cup of tiny cockles drenched in vinegar and black pepper. As an adult, I still walk into the fishing village for a paper cup of cockles, but they can also be found in supermarkets and at fishmongers too.

Serves 2

1 tablespoon oil

1 onion

1 clove of garlic

optional: 1 small red chilli

1 x 400g carton or tin of chopped tomatoes

a handful of fresh parsley, plus extra to garnish

1 x 150g jar of pickled cockles

160g spaghetti (or tagliatelle if one is feeling posh)

Put the oil into a medium-sized saucepan. Peel and finely slice the onion and garlic, and finely chop the chilli, if using. Add to the pan and cook on a medium heat for a few minutes.

When the onion starts to soften, pour over the chopped tomatoes and stir together. Finely chop the parsley and stir that into the tomatoey mixture in the pan.

Drain and thoroughly rinse the cockles, then add them to the pan. Stir and reduce the heat to a low simmer to thicken the sauce.

Meanwhile, bring a separate pot of water to the boil. Put in the spaghetti and cook according to the packet instructions, usually around 8 to 10 minutes. When the spaghetti is cooked, drain and toss with the cockles and sauce. Serve with extra chopped parsley to garnish.

TIP: Leftovers can be chilled in the fridge and served for next day's lunch, or warmed through for dinner.

BATTERED ANCHOVIES WITH QUICK TARTY SAUCE

When deep-frying food, such as these battered anchovies, I use a small milk pan with 5–7cm of oil in the bottom of it. The larger the pan you use, the more oil you will need. You can cook these in a frying pan with less oil but they are trickier, with more of a risk of burning yourself. As always when deep-frying, do it carefully!

Serves 4 as a snack or starter

oil, to deep-fry the fish

100g self-raising flour (or 100g plain flour and 1 level teaspoon baking powder or bicarbonate of soda)

a handful of fresh parsley

zest and juice of 1 lemon or 2 tablespoons bottled lemon juice

100ml milk

200ml natural yoghurt

100g fresh anchovy fillets

lemon wedges, to serve

First, pour 5cm depth of oil into a small deep-sided saucepan and put on a medium heat for 10 minutes. You want gentle bubbles rising to the surface – any more than that and there is a risk that it will hiss and spit at you and, although this recipe needs the oil to be hot in order to work, it doesn't need to be doing the haka in the pan. Besides, nobody likes a face full of hot oil – so be careful.

While the oil is heating, quickly make the batter. Tip the flour into a bowl, finely chop the parsley and scatter in – reserving a teaspoon or so for the tarty sauce. If you are using a fresh lemon, grate most of the zest in, but hold back a generous pinch or two with the parsley. Pour the milk in, add the lemon juice and mix well with a fork to make the batter. Set to one side. Some people swear by chilling the batter, so if you feel so inclined and you have space in the fridge, pop it in for a few minutes while you make the tarty sauce.

To make the sauce, simply stir the parsley and reserved lemon zest, if using, into the yoghurt, and mix well.

When the oil is hot, take the anchovies one at a time and dunk in the batter. Lift out with a tablespoon to keep as much batter as possible clinging to the little slivers of fish, and carefully lower into the oil. Repeat until the pan is three-quarters full, giving the batter space to expand without it all sticking together.

When each battered anchovy floats to the surface and is a crispy golden colour, remove it carefully with a slotted spoon and set on a baking tray covered with a clean non-fluffy tea towel or pieces of kitchen paper to drain the excess oil.

Repeat until all the anchovies are battered and cooked, then serve with a wedge of lemon and the tarty sauce.

SCAMPI ROES

The trick to making good batter is to get lots of air into it – I take a belt and braces approach of self-raising flour plus bicarbonate of soda or baking powder as well. The oil must be hot otherwise you will end up with a sodden mess of sad gloop dying at the bottom of your saucepan. When frying, I use a milk pan and pour in 5–7cm of oil, and fry in batches. If you are using a larger pan, you will inevitably use more oil. As always when deep-frying, do it carefully! If you have time, make the batter an hour or two early and chill it in the fridge. The reaction between hot oil and chilled batter makes for a light, crisp batter. These roes taste delicious served with traditional chips and peas. My Small Boy dips them in ketchup, because he's a toddler and everything goes with ketchup, and the softness of the roe makes them easy to eat for little mouths.

Serves 2

oil, to fry the roes

100g self-raising flour (or 100g plain flour and 1 level teaspoon baking powder or bicarbonate of soda), plus extra to flour the work surface

zest and juice of 1 lemon or 2 tablespoons bottled lemon juice

a scant teaspoon bicarbonate of soda

optional: 1 heaped teaspoon paprika

a handful of fresh parsley

100ml milk or 100ml water with a tablespoon of natural yoghurt

120g herring roes

lemon wedges, to serve

Pour oil into a small deep-sided saucepan to a depth of 5–7cm and put on a medium heat. Be careful of the hot oil!

Measure the flour into a mixing bowl and add the other dry ingredients: grate in the lemon zest, add the bicarbonate of soda and the paprika, if using. Finely chop the parsley, add to the bowl and mix everything together.

Pour in the milk – or water and yoghurt – add the lemon juice and mix in with a fork to form a smooth batter. Lightly flour your work surface and get everything ready for the battering and frying.

When the oil is gently bubbling, it's ready. Take a piece of herring roe, roll on the floured work surface and drop into the batter. Lift out with a tablespoon – to keep as much batter as possible clinging to the edges before the crucial frying process. Carefully lower it into the oil from the tablespoon. Repeat until the pan is two-thirds full, leaving room for the battered roe to expand without sticking together.

As each battered roe is floating and golden-crisp, lift out with a slotted spoon, draining any excess oil, and place on a plate to drain some more. Repeat until all of the roes are battered and cooked. Serve with lemon wedges.

TIP: Make a simple 'tarty' sauce to dunk the roes in by mixing natural yoghurt with lemon juice and chopped parsley.

You can replace the herring roes with any chunks of white fish to make little battered nuggets, but herring roe holds together well when cooked and makes for a pleasantly creamy smooth contrast to the crunchy batter.

SICILIAN-STYLE SARDINES WITH PASTA AND GREEN BEANS

Sardines are named after Sardinia, the Italian island where these fish were once plentiful. They can be bought fresh, but are commonly found in tins. Sardines come tinned in oil, brine or water – and any type will do for this recipe. The 120g portion is a guideline based on the typical tin size, not a hard and fast rule. If in doubt, tip the whole tin in. Sardines are a great source of vitamins and nutrients for busy adults and growing children alike, and this serving will provide almost all of a typical adult's daily requirement of vitamin B12 – second only to calf's liver and I know which I'd rather eat! They are also rich in calcium and vitamin D to promote healthy bones, protein for muscle growth and repair, and Omega-3 fats, which help to lower cholesterol levels.

Serves 2

160g pasta, such as spaghetti

1 x 120g tin of sardines

optional: 1 tablespoon oil
(if the sardines are preserved
in brine or water)

zest of 1 lemon

1 onion

1 clove of garlic

1 small red chilli or 2 pinches
of the dried stuff

a handful of raisins or sultanas

50g frozen green beans

finely chopped fresh parsley,
to garnish

Bring a saucepan of cold water to the boil. Pop in the pasta, turn down to a low heat and cooking according to the packet instructions, usually around 8 to 10 minutes.

While the pasta is boiling, drain the sardines. If they are preserved in oil, reserve the oil from the tin and put it into a small frying or sauté pan; if the sardines are in brine or water, discard the liquid and use normal vegetable oil in the pan. Finely grate most of the lemon zest into the pan – reserving some for a garnish. Peel and finely slice the onion and garlic, finely slice the chilli, and add to the oil and lemon zest. Tip in the raisins or sultanas and cook on a low heat until the onions are softening.

Put the green beans into the pan followed by the sardines, breaking up the fish gently with a wooden spoon or wooden fork so as not to scratch the protective coating on the pan.

Drain the pasta and tip into the pan with the fish and any reserved oil from the tin. Combine and serve with the lemon zest and parsley sprinkled over. Enjoy!

TIPS: You can substitute any green vegetable for the frozen green beans: spinach works well in this dish, as do peas and broccoli cut into small pieces.

For a slight variation, add chopped tomatoes to the onions – great if you like your pasta 'saucy'.

BIRDS

People are often surprised that I manage to eat meat on such a tight budget – but you'll notice that there aren't so many recipes in this chapter, as chicken and turkey are rare treats. I could easily substitute other ingredients, like chickpeas for example, instead.

However, there are some tricks I've learned along the way. I use turkey mince instead of minced pork, lamb or beef, flavouring it with a crumbled stock cube for more intensity when the recipe calls for it. I buy turkey legs, which are large, cumbersome things but pretty inexpensive – with a sharp knife and some elbow grease these yield a good deal of rich dark meat and a big bone for adding flavour to soups or stocks! I prefer thighs to any other cut from a chicken, since meat cooked on the bone has great flavour and is so juicy, but you can always substitute breast meat or legs in these recipes.

OVEN-BAKED FISH IN BEST TOMATO SAUCE WITH LEMON AND PARSLEY RICE

This simple recipe works well with most types of unsmoked fish. I use basa fillets (also called pangasius), pollock or cobbler as well as pilchards, or the occasional tin of sardines. To make it seasonal, use woody herbs like dried thyme or mixed dried herbs in the winter, and parsley or basil in the summer.

Serves 2

1 onion

1 x 400g carton or tin of chopped tomatoes

a fistful of fresh parsley, plus extra to garnish

a fistful of fresh basil, plus extra to garnish

zest and juice of ½ a lemon or 1 tablespoon bottled lemon juice

1 red chilli

200g white rice

1 tablespoon oil

240g white fish

TIP: To make this dish more quickly, simply put the fish into the roasting tin with all of the other ingredients except the rice, mix together to coat and cook in the preheated oven at 180°C/350°F/gas 4 for 20 minutes.

Preheat the oven to 150°C/300°F/gas 2.

First, prepare the tomato sauce. Peel and dice the onion and put into a saucepan with the chopped tomatoes. Place on a low heat and allow to simmer.

Pop the herbs into a tea cup and cut into them using kitchen scissors until they are finely chopped. Grate the lemon zest on top of the herbs, halve the lemon and squeeze the juice from one half in. Tip most of the herbs and lemon mixture into the tomatoes and onions in the pan, reserving a little for the rice. Chop the chilli and add it to the pan.

While the onions are gently softening in the tomatoes and the herbs are infusing the sauce, now would be a good time to pop the rice on to boil. Bring a saucepan of cold water to the boil, put in the rice and reduce to a simmer.

Brush a baking tray with the oil (to prevent the fish from sticking) then place the fish on to it, and bake in the preheated oven for 10 to 12 minutes. By this time, all being well, the rice should be nice and fluffy.

Drain any excess water from the rice and tip in the remaining lemon and herb mixture. Spoon on to plates or into bowls, and tip any excess juice or oil from the fish into the tomato sauce and give it a quick stir.

Serve the fish next to the rice and top generously with the tomato sauce. Garnish with extra herbs if available and enjoy the melty goodness.

TURKEY MEATBALLS

I love a good meatball and, to make these go further, I add mashed beans to the mix to pad them out. If you don't have hordes to feed on a budget, you can leave the beans out – but leftover meatballs can be tossed into a stew or kept in the fridge for a few days so don't be afraid to make a pile of them! Like with traditional Italian meatballs in tomato sauce, I suggest tipping some chopped tomatoes into the frying pan to heat through for 5 minutes along with the cooked meatballs at the end. You can then serve this atop a pile of spaghetti.

Makes approximately
20 meatballs

1 x 400g tin of baked beans or haricot beans

1 onion

1 chilli

1 slice of bread

a handful of fresh parsley

1 tablespoon flour, plus extra to shape the balls

500g turkey mince

2 tablespoons oil

Drain and rinse the beans, put into a small saucepan and cover with water. Bring to the boil, then reduce to a simmer and cook for 5 to 10 minutes until tender. Drain the beans and tip into a mixing bowl, then mash to a pulp.

Peel and finely chop the onion and finely chop the chilli, and toss into the mixing bowl with the bean pulp. Grate in the bread, finely chop the parsley and add that too. Add the flour and stir to combine. Add the mince and mix well with a wooden spoon or – as I prefer to do – use your hands.

With lightly floured hands to prevent sticking, form the mixture into balls. Around 1 tablespoon of mixture will make a decent-sized meatball. For little mouths, use a teaspoon – these also cook faster!

Fry the meatballs in the oil in a frying pan for 10 minutes on a medium heat, turning occasionally, until cooked through, then serve.

TIP: Make leftover meatballs into a delicious Greek stew by putting them into a pan with some rinsed and soaked white beans, chopped onion, a little paprika and chicken stock to cover. Add a sprinkling of fresh thyme leaves or mixed dried herbs. Simmer for 20 minutes on a medium heat and serve with mash or rice.

CHICKEN CHASSEUR

This one-pot special was originally surreptitiously scribbled down from a pullout in the *BBC Good Food* magazine in a doctor's waiting room, and has been adopted and adapted since into a classic comfort food. Depending on whether I've had friends round for dinner who have left half a bottle of wine or whether the well is running dry, sometimes I add more wine and less stock, sometimes I pour half a bottle in that's on the turn and reduce the amount of stock accordingly. The only rule is that the total liquid quantity must be 600ml. The older the wine is, the longer the stew will need to cook for. If there's no red in the house, use white wine for a lighter summery flavour, but I must confess I've never tried it with rosé. Serve with a pile of mash or rice and green vegetables.

Serves 4

1 onion

optional: 2 cloves of garlic

2 tablespoons oil

8 chicken thighs or 4 chicken legs

200g mushrooms

1 x 400g carton or tin of chopped tomatoes

250ml red wine

350ml chicken stock

a handful of woody herbs like thyme, sage or rosemary

Peel and finely slice the onion and garlic (if using), and put into a large non-stick saucepan with the oil on a low heat. Sweat gently until the onion starts to soften. Add the chicken, skin side down, and turn the heat up to medium to seal the meat, then turn over to brown the other side.

Brush any excess dirt from the mushrooms with a clean tea towel, break up into chunks and toss into the pot. Pour over the chopped tomatoes, wine and stock, and stir well to combine. Chop the herbs, add to the pot and crank the heat up to high. Bring to the boil, rapidly boil for 2 or 3 minutes, then reduce to a simmer. Cover and simmer for 20 minutes, until the chicken is cooked through.

Next you can simmer the stew gently, stirring, for another 30 to 60 minutes, to thicken the sauce and let the rich flavours develop, or you can remove the pan from the heat and allow it to stand, covered, for the same amount of time, to do pretty much the same job. If you have turned off the heat, put the pan back on and blast it through to heat before serving.

TIPS: For a great vegetarian alternative, leave out the chicken, use veggie stock rather than chicken and double the quantity of mushrooms to 400g.

Cut any leftover chicken off the bone and toss with pasta and leftover sauce for a quick, simple lunch that's packed with flavour.

EASY CHICKEN SATAY

Satay sauce is one of my favourite cheeky comforts – and I usually have the ingredients for it lying about. Traditional satay sauce uses coconut milk, but I substitute natural yoghurt and water, and a teaspoon of sugar if I feel the need. My satay takes just minutes to throw together and is a great standby for a quick and easy dinner. For a vegetarian alternative, serve it as a dipping sauce with vegetables instead of over chicken.

Serves 2

4 tablespoons oil

2 chicken breasts or 4 thighs or drumsticks

4 tablespoons peanut butter

1 small red chilli

optional: 1 teaspoon sugar

2 tablespoons natural yoghurt

Put the oil into a sauté or frying pan on a medium heat, then add the chicken and fry, turning occasionally, until browned all over and cooked through.

While the chicken is cooking, make the satay sauce. Combine the peanut butter and 240ml water in a small non-stick saucepan on a low heat, stirring to melt the peanut butter. Finely chop the chilli and add to the pan. Simmer on a low heat for a few minutes to soften the chilli and, if you want a slightly sweeter sauce, stir in the sugar.

Remove from the heat and stir the yoghurt through. Serve the sauce poured over the chicken.

CREAMY MUSTARD CHICKEN WITH WINTER VEG

This hearty, saucy dish is delicious in the winter, served with root vegetables and rice or mashed potatoes, or in the summer, with green vegetables and tossed over pasta. Any mustard will do for this – I keep English in the fridge, but wholegrain or any other sort will work fine. Use this recipe as a base, and adapt as you wish.

Serves 2

4 tablespoons oil

2 chicken breasts or 4 thighs or drumsticks

optional: 100g cooking or streaky bacon

1 onion

1 large carrot or 1 x 300g tin of carrots

1 teaspoon English, wholegrain or Dijon mustard

500ml chicken or vegetable stock

a handful of fresh parsley

a handful of fresh thyme

200ml double cream or natural yoghurt

Heat the oil in a medium-sized non-stick saucepan and put in the chicken. If using thighs, drumsticks or breasts with skin on, place them in skin side down. Cook for 5 minutes on each side on a medium heat to seal. If using bacon, chop it into 1cm chunks and toss into the pot with the chicken.

Peel and chop the onion and wash and slice the carrot, and add to the pan. If using tinned carrots, simply drain and tip in. Stir the mustard into the stock and pour into the pan to cover the vegetables and half-cover the chicken. Finely chop the parsley and thyme and add to the pot. Cover with a lid and cook for 20 to 30 minutes, until the chicken is cooked through.

Remove the chicken and stir the cream into the sauce in the pan. Boil rapidly for a few minutes to thicken the sauce. If you've got yoghurt rather than cream, add it off the heat after reducing the sauce.

Serve the chicken with the sauce poured over.

TIPS: Green beans make a great addition to this dish – in fact, chuck in any vegetables that are kicking around. As a rule of thumb, add root veg shortly after browning the chicken and add small veg like peas, shredded greens or green beans 5 minutes before serving. For a vegetarian version, just leave out the chicken and put in more veg as required.

SPANISH-STYLE CHICKEN

This is another 'what's in the cupboard?' recipe, inspired by a chicken and chorizo dish in Nigella Lawson's *Kitchen* cookbook, but rustled up instead with a tin of mandarins, some paprika and chicken. I've made it with a carton of chopped tomatoes thrown over the top for more of a casserole dish, but it's lovely as it is, served with a pile of fluffy rice or potato wedges, or a simple side of green vegetables.

Serves 2

4 chicken thighs or 6 drumsticks

2 tablespoons oil

1 onion

2 cloves of garlic

1 x 200g tin of mandarins in juice

1 heaped tablespoon paprika

a handful of fresh basil
or parsley

First, put the chicken skin side down in a frying pan with the oil, and cook on a medium heat for a few minutes on each side to seal. Peel and finely slice the onion, peel and crush the garlic, and add to the pan to soften.

Next make the marinade. In a large mug or medium-sized bowl, mix the mandarins – and their juice – with the paprika. Finely chop the herbs and mix through. Pour over the chicken in the pan.

Cook on a medium heat, turning the chicken a few times and spooning the marinade over, for around 30 minutes or until the chicken is cooked. To check that the chicken is cooked, insert a sharp knife into the fattest part and see that the flesh is white, not pink, and that the juices run clear.

TIPS: Leftover chicken can be stripped from the bone, mixed with leftover sauce and 1–2 tablespoons yoghurt, then stuffed into a pitta bread or wrap for the next day's lunch. Alternatively mix leftovers with a carton of chopped tomatoes and heat through to make a casserole.

To make this a one-pot meal, add some diced new potatoes in with the onion – tinned ones work extremely well with this dish, and are also in keeping with the store cupboard ingredients.

DIET-COKE CHICKEN

You don't have to use Diet Coke to make this barbecue sauce – regular 'full-fat' Coke will work just fine too. I use supermarket own-brand cola, so feel free to use any brand you like or have to hand. Serve this sticky deliciousness with rice, chips, couscous or another carbohydrate of your choice to soak up the sauce.

Serves 2

2 tablespoons oil

4 chicken thighs or 6 drumsticks

1 x 330ml can of Diet Coke

1 x 400g carton or tin of chopped tomatoes

½ teaspoon English, Dijon or wholegrain mustard

a few sprigs of fresh parsley, to serve

Put the oil into a saucepan and pop the chicken in skin side down on a medium heat to brown for 10 minutes, turning halfway through to seal the other side. Then pour the Diet Coke over the chicken and crank up to a high heat to bring to the boil. Boil vigorously for a few minutes.

Pour over the chopped tomatoes, add the mustard, reduce the heat to medium and stir well to mix the sauce. Cook for 30 minutes on a low to medium heat, stirring frequently to prevent the sauce from burning.

When the chicken is cooked through, remove from the heat. Serve with lashings of the sweet, sticky sauce and some parsley sprinkled over.

TIP: Replace the cola with a fizzy orange drink or natural orange juice for a sweet, fruity sauce similar to sweet and sour.

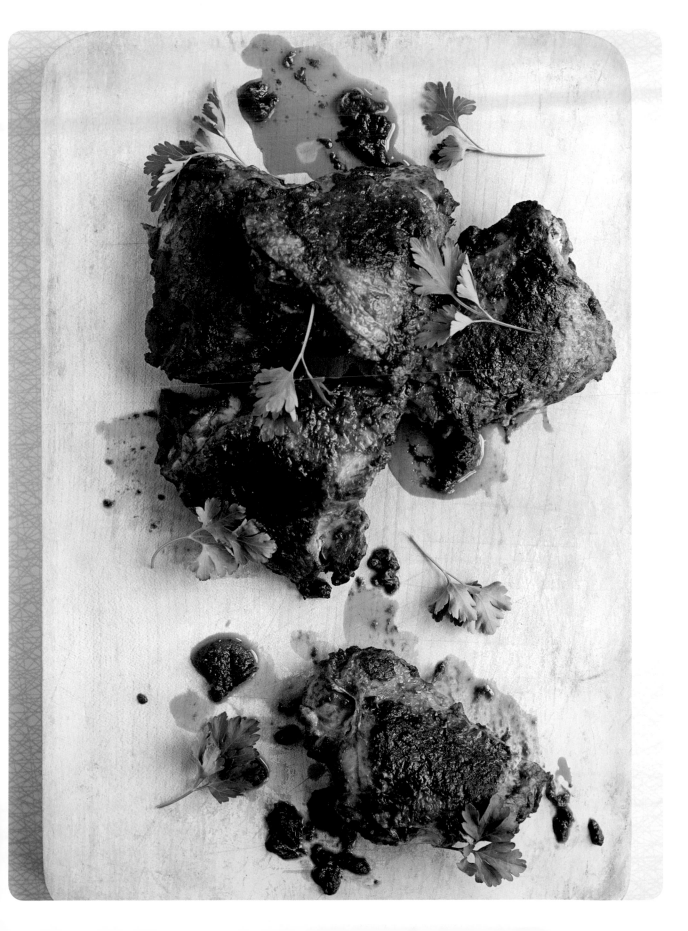

PIGGY

Look out for packets of bacon called 'cooking bacon' – the term makes me smile, as what else is bacon for other than for cooking? These packets are a bit of a bacon roulette: some contain large chunks, perfect for casseroles like Spring Piggy (see page 176), and some contain little scraps suitable only for risottos (see Brie and Bacon Risotto on page 102) or potato or pasta salads. Sometimes you'll get really lucky and have a large steaky piece packed in with all the little scrappy bits.

I always rinse cooking bacon thoroughly before using it, to rinse off any excess salt, and trim off any excess fat with a sharp knife or kitchen scissors. When I buy a pack, the first thing I do is open it up, separate the bacon into 'chunks' and 'scraps' and cook accordingly.

HONEY AND MUSTARD GLAZED GAMMON JOINT WITH APPLE SAUCE

This is a special treat recipe, but I can usually make it into dinner for two nights, plus a soup or casserole from the leftovers, so it's definitely good value. You can even use the cooking liquid as well as any leftover meat – see the tip below! The apples are optional, but are a good way to use up the roasting juices and some of the onions. If you have no apples, fish out the onions from the stock, add them to the roasting dish and serve that way instead.

Serves 6

2 onions

1 carrot

1 x 750g gammon joint

6 apples

2 sprigs of fresh thyme

a drizzle of oil

3 tablespoons honey

3 teaspoons wholegrain mustard

TIPS: Keep the cooking liquid and unused cooked onions, and blitz with a can of mushy peas to make a delicious ham and pea soup. Garnish with shredded gammon if there is any left over.

Alternatively, use the cooking liquid to make a casserole. Simply add some chunks of leftover gammon, cooked peas or green beans and a carton or tin of chopped tomatoes, and reheat for a gorgeous next-day dinner.

Peel and quarter the onions and wash and roughly chop the carrot. Put both into a saucepan large enough to contain the gammon with space around. Place the gammon joint on top of the vegetables, pop the apples (left whole) around it, add the thyme sprigs and cover with water.

Bring to the boil, then simmer on a medium heat for 30 minutes to cook the meat. If using a larger or smaller joint of gammon, the rule of thumb is 20 minutes per 500g. A little before the end of the boiling time, preheat the oven to 180°C/350°F/gas 4.

When cooked, place the gammon in a roasting tin lined with foil (to catch the roasting juices) and a drizzle of oil. Remove the apples and half the onions and set to one side to make the apple sauce. Fish out the sprigs of thyme and discard. Reserve the cooking liquid and remaining vegetables for another dish.

In a small bowl or a mug, mix the honey and mustard with a tablespoon of the hot stock to soften the honey.

Cut away the rind from the gammon with a sharp knife, leaving as much of the fat behind as possible. Score the fat in a diamond shape by making diagonal slashes one way, then crossing back over the top. Pour the honey and mustard glaze over the gammon, and pop the apples around it in the roasting dish. Roast in the preheated oven for 20 minutes, until the fat is golden.

Allow the meat to rest for 5 minutes before carving. Halve the apples and scrape out the soft flesh, discarding any pips, and chop up the reserved onions. Mix the apple flesh, chopped onions and roasting juices to make a delicious sauce.

PORK KOKKINISTO

This traditional Cypriot dish is best served with light, fluffy rice or potatoes and green vegetables. It can be cooked in the oven in a roasting tin (25 to 30 minutes at 180°C/350°F/ gas 4) or on the hob in a large frying pan or sauté pan, depending on what you have available to use. It is delicious made with pork belly, pork loin or spare ribs, or even chicken thighs and drumsticks if you fancy them. The sauce can be made separately as a standby for a quick Bolognese or pasta sauce – this is one of my go-to recipes, when I want something rich and comforting, but with only a little lazy effort.

Serves 4

600g pork belly or pork loin

2 tablespoons oil

1 large onion

200ml red wine

1 x 400g carton or tin of chopped tomatoes

3 sprigs of fresh rosemary or 2 teaspoons mixed dried herbs

1 tablespoon sugar

a handful of fresh parsley

Cut the pork into large cubes, around 5cm by 5cm. Pop into a frying pan, skin side down, with the oil on a medium heat for a few minutes to seal. Turn over to seal all the edges of the meat, then reduce the heat to low.

Peel and finely slice the onion, and add to the pan. Sweat on a low heat for a few minutes until it starts to soften.

Pour in the wine and turn the heat up slightly to medium to simmer the meat. Tip in the tomatoes. Finely chop the rosemary and add to the pan with the sugar. Stir to combine the ingredients, and leave to simmer, uncovered, on a low heat for 20 minutes or until the meat is cooked.

Finely chop the parsley and sprinkle over to serve.

PORK AND BEANS CASSOULET

There's no duck in this budget version of the popular restaurant classic, but I don't really miss it. You can eat my cassoulet with mash, or toss some cooked diced new potatoes in along with the beans for a one-pot comfort dish to eat from a deep bowl in a corner of the sofa on a Friday night. Tinned carrots work just fine for this, by the way, but add them at the same time as the chopped tomatoes, because they take less time to cook.

Serves 4

a splash of oil

8 sausages

1 onion

1 large carrot

2 cloves of garlic

100g bacon, chopped

a handful of fresh herbs –
parsley, rosemary or thyme
will do

zest and juice of ½ a lemon or
1 tablespoon bottled lemon juice

1 chicken stock cube, dissolved
in 400ml boiling water

200g tinned chopped tomatoes
(half a standard-sized carton
or tin)

1 x 400g tin of haricot beans
(or baked beans with the
sauce rinsed off)

Put the oil into a large frying pan or sauté pan, prick the sausages and pop them into the pan on a medium heat. Cook for around 10 minutes, until the sausages start to brown, turning them to cook all over. Meanwhile, peel and slice the onion, and wash and slice or dice the carrot. Peel and finely slice the garlic, or crush in a garlic crusher if you have one available. Add these to the pan.

When the sausages are sealed, remove from the pan and allow to cool before cutting into 1cm thick slices. Put the sausage slices back into the pan, along with the bacon, and stir well to mix with the vegetables.

Finely chop the herbs and add to the pan. Grate in the lemon zest, add the lemon juice and stir well. Pour over the stock and chopped tomatoes and stir again. Leave to simmer for 15 minutes to cook the vegetables and develop the flavours.

Drain and thoroughly rinse the tinned beans, add to the pan and stir together. Turn the heat up high for a few minutes to heat the beans through and slightly reduce the sauce. Serve hot.

TIPS: To make this dish extra special, add a glass of white wine and a crumbled chicken stock cube in place of the stock – but you'll also need to pour in some boiling water to make the liquid quantity up to 400ml.

Use chicken thighs, drumsticks or cut up chicken breast instead of the sausages. Make sure to completely seal the meat on all sides before adding the stock.

This is one of those dishes that improves with time, so keep any leftovers in an airtight container in the fridge to toss with cooked pasta for next day's lunch or dinner.

OH MY GOD DINNER

This dish started off as a late-night cry of, 'Oh my God, dinner!' since I had been working late and lost track of time – and meals. A quick rummage in the fridge turned up some cooking bacon and a sad piece of Brie, and Oh My God Dinner was born.

Serves 2

100g bacon

juice of ½ a lemon or 1 tablespoon bottled lemon juice

1 courgette, diced

1 small red chilli, finely chopped

150g spaghetti

50g fresh or frozen green beans

a fistful of fresh parsley

a fistful of fresh basil

1 clove of garlic

30g Brie cheese, or a chunk (if like me you really don't weigh things like that)

Put a saucepan of water on to boil. Chop the bacon into small pieces and put into a large sauté pan with the lemon juice, diced courgette and chopped chilli. Cook on a low heat, stirring occasionally to turn the ingredients.

In the meantime, pop the spaghetti, broken in half, into the boiling water and simmer according to the packet instructions (usually around 8 to 10 minutes). After about 4 or 5 minutes, add the green beans to the water for the final few minutes of cooking.

Put the herbs into a tea cup, bowl or other small receptacle and chop finely with kitchen scissors. Peel and finely chop or crush the garlic and stir into the chopped herbs. Dice the Brie and keep it aside.

When the spaghetti is cooked, drain and tip into the sauté pan containing the bacon and courgettes. Stir the herbs and garlic through, and add the diced Brie. Remove the pan from the heat and toss everything together – the Brie will melt slightly to form an almost sauce.

SPRING PIGGY

This is an adaptation of a Nigella Lawson recipe for spring chicken, made instead with chunks of gammon or cooking bacon. I don't peel my veg – a quick but intense rinse usually does the trick and there's so much goodness just under the skins of vegetables that it's a shame to waste it. I use yoghurt in this dish rather than any kind of cream because it is one of my food shop staples. Serve Spring Piggy with mash, rice or bread. It is also delicious tossed through spaghetti – in fact it works with most carbs!

Serves 4

300g cooking or streaky bacon

1 onion

1 clove of garlic

a splash of oil

100ml white wine

a fistful of fresh thyme, chopped

a fistful of fresh parsley, chopped

1 carrot

1 chicken stock cube, dissolved in 500ml boiling water

1 teaspoon English mustard

70g Savoy cabbage or spring greens (about a quarter of a medium cabbage)

50g fresh or frozen green beans

optional: 2 tablespoons natural yoghurt

Dice the bacon, peel and chop the onion, and peel and finely slice the garlic. Put these into a large sauté pan on a low heat, with a splash of oil. Once the onion has softened, add the wine and the chopped thyme and parsley, stir through and leave simmering on a low heat.

Wash and chop the carrot, and add it to the pan. Pour in the hot chicken stock and stir in the mustard. Cover and leave to simmer on a low heat for 20 minutes, checking and stirring occasionally, as you see fit.

Wash and finely chop the cabbage or shred the greens and, about 5 minutes before serving, add to the pan along with the green beans. Right at the end of cooking, stir the yoghurt through to make the sauce slightly creamy – this is optional but delicious.

TIPS: It's hard to improve on this, but try it with any root veg you have to hand. Peeled and chopped sweet potato, baby turnips, swede and parsnips all work well along with or instead of the carrot.

Add more yoghurt for extra creamy richness or, if you're feeling flush, a little crème fraîche or cream work beautifully too.

Add some diced chicken at the same time as the bacon, or chicken thighs on the bone à la Nigella – just remember to seal the meat on all sides before adding the wine and stock!

This will keep in the fridge for a few days or in the freezer for about 3 months. If freezing, add a little extra water to the sauce to allow it to coat the bacon and veg – this helps it to freeze better.

SAUSAGE AND BEER CASSEROLE

I love sausages. I especially love how the cheapest can of beer can be enriched by half a dozen sausages and a few other ingredients for a home-comfort classic dinner that's delicious with a pile of mash and some green veg.

Serves 2

6 sausages

a splash of oil

1 onion

1 clove of garlic

200g fresh or tinned mushrooms (drained weight)

1 x 330ml can of beer

1 x 400g carton or tin of chopped tomatoes

a handful of fresh thyme or parsley, chopped

Prick the sausages, put into a medium non-stick saucepan with the oil and cook on a medium heat. Meanwhile, peel and slice the onion and garlic, then add to the pan.

If you're using fresh mushrooms, clean and slice them; if you're using tinned ones, drain them. When the sausages have browned all over, add the mushrooms and continue cooking for a few minutes. Then pour in the beer and chopped tomatoes, add the herbs and stir everything together.

Reduce the heat to low and cook for 30 minutes, stirring occasionally to prevent it sticking to the bottom of the pan.

TIPS: To make this go further, add a tin of white beans. I rinse the sauce from a can of baked beans, but any tinned white beans – haricot, cannelini, butter beans – will do.

Replace the beer with red or white wine if you have it – red wine for a deep, rich flavour, white for a lighter, sweeter dish.

HAM, PEA AND MINT CASSEROLE

This delicious ham casserole is adapted from a favourite old recipe of mine – where I would boil the ham joint whole to make a stock, before shredding it into the casserole. This faster version is no compromise, making a delicious hearty dinner in less than half the time. For an extra special twist, serve with crusty bread topped with melted cheese and green vegetables.

Serves 4

1 x 500g uncooked ham joint or 500g bacon

2 onions

1 tablespoon oil

300ml chicken stock

100ml white wine

a generous handful of fresh parsley

a generous handful of fresh mint

500g small white potatoes or 500g tinned potatoes (drained weight)

150g frozen peas

Dice the ham or bacon and peel and chop the onions. Put into a frying pan with the oil and fry on a medium heat, turning to seal the meat on all sides. Leave to cook through for about 20 minutes, stirring occasionally.

Meanwhile, pour the stock and wine into a saucepan and bring to a simmer. Finely chop the parsley and mint, including the stalks, and add to the pan. Wash and dice the potatoes, leaving the skins on (or drain if using tinned ones), and put into the saucepan. Cook until the vegetables are tender, around 10 minutes for fresh veg or 5 minutes for tinned.

Once they're done, remove about half the potatoes from the saucepan and place in a blender. Add just enough of the stock to cover, and blend until smooth. Tip back into the pan and stir through.

When the ham or bacon is cooked, toss everything in the frying pan into the saucepan along with the frozen peas. Stir and cook through for a few final minutes until the peas are tender, then serve.

TIP: To bulk out or sweeten the casserole add 2 large carrots or 200g tinned carrots (drained weight), chopped, at the same time as the potatoes.

BEST MACARONI WITH BACON AND SPINACH

Simple macaroni cheese is delicious comfort food, but macaroni cheese made with bacon and spinach is something else entirely! A cross between carbonara and a traditional macaroni cheese, this recipe is easily doubled to make a warm and filling dinner for friends. Use Cheddar or any Italian hard cheese in this dish – supermarkets often sell a value range pretend version of Parmesan that is perfect.

Serves 2

160g macaroni or penne pasta

2 tablespoons oil

1 fat clove of garlic

100g bacon

1 tablespoon flour

250ml milk

¼ teaspoon English mustard (but wholegrain or Dijon will do, if that's what you have to hand)

2 handfuls of fresh spinach leaves or 1 x 400g tin of spinach

a handful of fresh parsley

50g hard strong cheese, grated

First, put a saucepan of water on to boil, add the pasta and reduce to a medium heat for 8 to 10 minutes to cook (or follow the packet instructions).

Meanwhile, gently heat the oil in a non-stick saucepan on a medium heat. Peel and finely chop the garlic, cut the bacon into small pieces and put into the pan. Once the bacon has coloured, add the flour and stir in quickly to form a thick paste. Add a splash of milk and mix well with a fork or wooden spoon until fully combined. Repeat, gradually stirring in the milk little by little to form a white sauce, then add the mustard and reduce the heat to very low.

Chop the spinach and the parsley together in a mug or small bowl. If you are using tinned spinach, drain it and chop separately. Add both to the sauce and stir in well. Then tip the grated cheese into the sauce, stirring until it is melted.

Drain the pasta, toss with the bacon, spinach and cheese sauce and serve immediately.

TIP: For a more traditional macaroni cheese, pour the finished pasta and sauce mixture into an ovenproof dish and bake in the oven for 20 minutes at 180°C/350°F/gas 4.

MUSHROOM, BACON AND ALE CASSEROLE

The star of this hearty winter dinner is a can of cheap bitter ale, cooked with the onions, bacon vegetables and herbs to make a rich winter casserole. If you don't have any bitter to hand, use beef or chicken stock instead. I made a small portion of soup – try the Really Tomatoey Basilly Soup (see page 44) – using up the remaining 'halves' of all of the vegetables listed below. You can also use what's left of the can of bitter to make Beer and Sultana Bread (see page 30). Serve with mash and green veg.

Serves 2

½ an onion

1 clove of garlic

100g cooking or streaky bacon

optional: a splash of oil

260ml bitter

½ a potato

½ a carrot

50g mushrooms

1 beef stock cube

a fistful of fresh thyme

Peel and chop the onion and garlic. Put into a sauté pan or heavy-bottomed saucepan. Chop the bacon into small pieces. I cut mine to the size of tiny pancetta squares, but it's up to you. Add to the pan and cook over a medium-high heat, stirring constantly to make sure nothing sticks to the pan. You can add oil as an optional extra but I prefer to do without, since a little fat seeps out of the bacon, also making this cheaper.

When the bacon is sealed (the outside edges are cooked and no raw bits of bacon are poking through), pour over the bitter. Wash and chop the potato and carrot. Gently clean any excess earth from the mushrooms with a clean tea towel and slice them up. Add all the vegetables to the pan. Crumble in the stock cube, add the thyme leaves and pour in water to cover.

Allow to simmer for 30 minutes, covered, stirring occasionally, then serve.

TIPS: Add ½ a 400g carton or tin of chopped tomatoes instead of the water for a more hearty base. Vegetarians can also omit the bacon and replace the beef stock with vegetable stock.

Play around with the herbs. This stew would also work well with bay leaves, rosemary, parsley, sage or a combination of whatever you have growing on your windowsill.

FIRECRACKER SAUSAGES WITH TRAGEDY MASH

'If you ever see me eating sweet potato mash out of a saucepan, you know it's bad news', is a phrase that most of my friends are familiar with. Sweet potato mash with chilli and cheese is my go-to tragedy food, spooned straight from the saucepan whilst watching many a re-run of *Bridget Jones's Diary*. It's simple, sweet, quick and comforting. Here I've topped it with another favourite – firecracker sausages. If the double chilli hit is too much, eliminate it from the sausages but keep it in the mash. The quantities given here are easily doubled to make this for 2 people.

Serves 1

1 large sweet potato

1 large white potato

2–3 sausages

a splash of oil

1 small or ½ a large onion

2 small red chillies

1 tablespoon white wine vinegar

1 tablespoon marmalade

1 teaspoon wholegrain mustard or scant ¼ teaspoon English mustard

a handful of grated hard strong cheese, to taste

Bring a medium saucepan of water to the boil. Wash and roughly chop the sweet potato and white potato, and put into the pan. Reduce the heat to a medium simmer and leave on a back hob to cook for 20 minutes.

Meanwhile, prick the sausages and put them into a medium-sized frying pan or sauté pan with the oil. Peel and slice the onion – think chunkyish slices like hot dog onions! – and add them to the pan. Once the onions have softened, add 1 finely sliced chilli, the vinegar, marmalade and mustard, and cook on a medium heat, stirring to encourage the onions to absorb all of the spicy sweet flavours and turning the sausages to brown and cook through.

When the potatoes are soft, drain them, leaving them slightly wet to mash. Finely slice the remaining chilli and toss it into the potato pan along with the grated cheese. Mash with a fork or potato masher according to desired consistency – I like mine a bit rough and chunky.

Spoon the mash into a bowl, top with the spicy sausages and onions, and enjoy.

SAUSAGE AND LENTIL ONE-POT DINNER

This hearty dinner may seem as though it has a lot of ingredients, but most of them are useful store cupboard staples that form the basis of many of my recipes. The bacon isn't essential, so if you don't have it don't worry too much, just add a couple of extra sausages.

Serves 4

1 tablespoon oil

6 sausages

100g cooking or streaky bacon, chopped

1 carrot or 100g tinned carrots

2 large white potatoes or 400g tinned potatoes

1 onion

2 sprigs of fresh thyme or rosemary

150g dried red or brown lentils

1 x 400g carton or tin of chopped tomatoes

400ml vegetable, beef or chicken stock

First, heat the oil in a large frying pan, sauté pan or non-stick saucepan. Prick the sausages and add to the pan along with the chopped bacon, and sizzle together on a low heat for a few minutes to brown the sausages.

Wash and roughly chop the carrot and potatoes (or drain if using tinned). Peel and chop the onion. Add the vegetables to the pan, stirring to soften the onions. Chop the rosemary or thyme and add to the pan. Tip in the lentils and chopped tomatoes, and pour in the stock to cover.

Bring to the boil and boil rapidly for a few minutes, then reduce the heat to medium and simmer for 25 minutes, or until the lentils are tender and the sausages are cooked through.

TIPS: Allow leftovers to cool and freeze in an airtight container for up to 3 months.

Replace the lentils with a tin of white beans for a hearty sausage and bean casserole.

HAGGIS-STYLE MEATBALLS

I used this recipe a few years ago on Burns Night to make individual 'haggises' from lamb mince for squeamish friends who didn't want the real thing. Those of us who wanted real haggis happily tucked in, and those who didn't enjoyed these chunks of peppery, oaty meat steamed in pudding tins instead. I have since remade them as meatballs using pork, lamb or turkey mince, which are delicious with mash and gravy, or eaten cold from the fridge as a snack. As a nod to tradition, you should really serve them with 'neeps and tatties' (mash made from part potato and part swede) and shredded cabbage or spring greens.

Serves 4–6

1 red onion

25g oats

a pinch of ground cinnamon

black pepper, to taste

a handful of fresh sage or parsley

500g pork mince (or turkey, lamb or beef mince)

optional: 1 egg, beaten

flour, to shape the meatballs

2 tablespoons oil

Peel and chop the onion very finely and put into a mixing bowl. Add the oats, cinnamon and plenty of black pepper. Finely chop the sage or parsley and add to the bowl. Tip in the mince, then mix well with your hands or a wooden spoon to combine the mixture. If it doesn't 'pack' together well, add the egg or a splash of water to moisten the mixture.

With floured hands, take about a tablespoon of the mixture and shape into a ball. Repeat with the rest of the mixture. Heat the oil in a frying pan and fry the meatballs on a medium heat for around 10 minutes, turning occasionally, until cooked through. Depending on the size of your pan, you may need to do this in batches.

TIP: The meatballs will keep in the fridge (cooked or uncooked) for up to 3 days, or you can freeze them uncooked in an airtight container then allow to defrost naturally and fry as above.

SWEETS AND TREATS

Dessert is by no means essential at the end of every dinnertime. However, simple sweet treats like My Cakeys (see page 192) and Queen of Hearts Jam Tarts (see page 206) are not only delicious, but also making them can be an ideal activity to keep Small Boys and Small Girls occupied on rainy days and Sundays.

I've recreated some childhood favourites here, like School Dinner Days Jam Swiss Roll (see page 194). And I've given my own twist to the classic crumble by adding beer to make the Beery Berry Crumble (see page 205). All the while I still use basic, low-cost ingredients in my recipes.

WHITE CHOCOLATE AND PEACH TRAYBAKE

This was initially a use-up recipe for half a tin of peaches I had lurking around in the fridge following making a smaller quantity of my Peach and Chickpea Curry (see page 74), but has grown since then into something I'll make for its own sake. It's a homely traybake that keeps for days in an airtight container and can be popped into lunchboxes and picnics, or idly nibbled on during the day.

Serves 6–8

250g butter, plus extra to grease the cake tin

200g sugar

3 eggs

200g tinned peaches (drained weight)

100g white chocolate

200g self-raising flour (or 200g plain flour and 1 heaped teaspoon baking powder or bicarbonate of soda)

Preheat the oven to 180°C/350°F/gas 4 and lightly grease a 20 x 20cm square cake tin or small roasting tin.

Cream the butter and sugar together in a mixing bowl with a fork or wooden spoon until well combined. Break in the eggs and mix together, beating until smooth.

Drain the peaches and chop into chunks – fine chunks will ensure a subtle distribution of fruit throughout the traybake, but larger chunks give a delightful sweet, juicy bite. Add to the mixing bowl and stir through. Using a sharp knife, chop the chocolate into small chunks – or you can put it in a freezer bag and bash it into chunks with a rolling pin – and fold into the mixture. Add the flour, and bicarbonate of soda or baking powder, if using, and mix well to combine into a soft, sweet-smelling batter.

Pour the batter into the tin and bake in the centre of the preheated oven for around 45 minutes – depending on the size of your tin. A shallow tin will cook faster, whereas a deeper tin will take its time. To check, insert a sharp knife into the centre of the cake. If the knife comes out clean, the traybake is ready.

Allow to cool in the tin for 10 minutes before turning out and chopping into squares.

TIPS: To make a Bakewell-style traybake, use fresh raspberries instead of the tinned peaches and replace 50g of the sugar with ground almonds.

Instead of the peaches you can use apricots, mandarins or berries – anything you fancy really.

MY CAKEYS

This definitely doesn't class as a recipe, more something cheap, fun and edible to make with the kids. Cornflakes and peanut butter were staple ingredients of my original £10-a-week food shop, and these treats were the product of a rainy day at home with a toddler and a desire for something sweet and delicious. Small Boy called them 'My Cakeys', hence the name. Life without treats and sweets and cakes is a bit rubbish, and at such a low cost it's a fun way to introduce the kids to the magic of cooking as well. There are also many variations to the humble cornflake cake – try the options given in the tips below for starters.

Makes 30 cornflake cakes

100g white chocolate

1 tablespoon peanut butter

50g cornflakes

Break the chocolate up into a medium-sized microwaveable bowl. Add the peanut butter. Put the bowl in the microwave on low or defrost setting for 2 minutes. It should all melt. Do NOT put it in the microwave on a high setting to make it melt faster. White chocolate goes quite funny if heated too fast – it sort of thickens with a nasty burnt, sour smell.

Stir the melted white chocolate and peanut butter together until well mixed and an even colour.

Crush the cornflakes into the bowl a handful at a time and stir in. Keep adding cornflakes until you can't coat them all any more in the chocolate and peanut butter mixture. Spoon heaped teaspoon-sized dollops on to a very lightly greased baking tray or on to baking paper.

Allow to set. If you want them quickly, pop the tray in the fridge for 10 minutes.

TIPS: The cornflake cakes will keep in an airtight container for about 4 days.

Try dark chocolate with honey instead of white chocolate and peanut butter. Or try milk chocolate with peanut butter for something that isn't quite a Ferrero Rocher, but comes pretty darn close.

CHOCOLATE BUTTONS

I make these as lovely, simple gifts for people, for the price of a bar of value range chocolate and an embellishment of your choice. Grown-up versions can have some lavender buds and lemon zest on white chocolate, chilli flakes or chopped fresh mint on dark chocolate, or orange zest on milk chocolate. For Easter, I add a drop of green food colouring to white chocolate and press a small sugar flower into the centre – the possibilities are endless. My Small Boy loves to help me decorate these – and eat them afterwards, of course!

Makes approximately
12 large buttons

100g white, milk or dark chocolate

embellishments of your choice: hundreds and thousands, sugar balls, coloured sugar crystals, orange or lemon zest, chopped fresh herbs – run wild!

Lay a sheet of greaseproof paper on a baking tray.

Fill a small saucepan one-third full of water and bring it to the boil. Put a heatproof mixing bowl on top of the pan and then carefully lift it off, to check that the water is not touching the bottom of the bowl. If the water is touching the bowl, tip a little away. (If the water touches the bowl while the chocolate is heating, the chocolate will become bitter.) Break up the chocolate and put it into the bowl to melt, reducing the heat to a simmer. Stir the melting chocolate regularly. Hold the side of the mixing bowl with a tea towel or oven glove, as it will get hot. If you are making this with children, you can melt the chocolate in a microwave on a low heat instead of on top of the stove.

When the chocolate has melted, drop a tablespoon of it onto the baking paper, using the back of the spoon to spread it into a circle shape. Add your embellishments while the chocolate is still melted, and repeat until all the chocolate has been used up.

Allow to set – which can be speeded up by popping the tray in the fridge for a few minutes – and carefully remove from the greaseproof paper.

SCHOOL DINNER DAYS JAM SWISS ROLL

This is a favourite recipe of mine, a school days classic, and easy to make with small children as well. My small boy loves spreading the filling on this one with the back of a spoon and a little supervision – and it keeps in the fridge for a few days, well wrapped. For an American version, use a mixture of peanut butter and jam instead of just red jam.

Serves 4–6

4 eggs

100g sugar, plus 2 tablespoons for the filling

100g self-raising flour (or 100g plain flour and 1 level teaspoon baking powder or bicarbonate of soda)

150ml natural yoghurt

4 heaped tablespoons set red jam

optional: sugar, to serve

Preheat the oven to 180°C/350°F/gas 4.

Break the eggs into a mixing bowl and pour in the sugar. Beat together with a fork until the eggs are lighter in colour. Add the flour and mix until well combined.

Line a large roasting dish with greaseproof paper, grease the paper lightly and then spread the mixture in. Cook in the preheated oven for 5 minutes, until golden.

Take the sponge out of the oven and let it cool a little. Meanwhile pour the yoghurt and the sugar for the filling into a large bowl and whip into soft peaks with a fork. Spoon the jam into a mug or small bowl and add 2 tablespoons water. Mix well to loosen the jam, then gently fold into the whipped yoghurt.

Spread the sponge thickly with the flavoured yoghurt. Carefully roll up the sponge and topping to form the Swiss roll, very carefully peeling off the greaseproof paper as you go. If you like, sprinkle with sugar to serve. You can eat it immediately still slightly warm, or refrigerate and enjoy cold.

TIP: For a decadent version, you can use double cream instead of the yoghurt and sugar in the filling – yay! Make this with marmalade, lemon curd, really anything you like spread inside the Swiss roll.

PADDINGTON BEAR SPONGE PUDDINGS

These were inspired by a little lost bear in a blue duffel coat, reminiscent of my childhood. As well as marmalade sandwiches, which are a comfortable and unapologetic staple in my busy household, marmalade puddings can be eaten warm and cosy with custard, or cold as lunchtime snacks.

Makes 6 small puddings or 4 large ones

70g butter, plus extra to grease the muffin tins

50g sugar

a splash of lemon juice

2 eggs

100g self-raising flour (or 100g plain flour and 1 level teaspoon baking powder or bicarbonate of soda)

8 heaped teaspoons marmalade, plus extra to serve

Preheat the oven to 170°C/325°F/gas 3.

Place the butter in a microwaveable dish and heat on the defrost setting for 30 seconds until soft. Transfer to a large mixing bowl. Add the sugar and lemon juice, and cream together until well combined. Break the eggs in, then add the flour. Mix well with a fork or wooden spoon to create a smooth, glossy batter.

Lightly grease each of your muffin tins with a little extra butter to stop the puddings sticking to the sides – which will ruin a seriously good dessert! Dollop a generous blob of marmalade in the bottom of each tin. Divide the batter among the tins, spooning it on top of the marmalade until each tin is approximately two-thirds full.

Cook in the centre of the preheated oven for 30 minutes. The puddings should be risen, light and golden, and should come away from the tin easily.

Serve with extra marmalade warmed through to make a sticky sauce!

TIPS: Add ginger for a gentle kick – stir either a meagre teaspoon of ground ginger or a little grated fresh ginger into the batter.

Try substituting jam or lemon curd for the marmalade to make light, sticky fruity or lemony puddings. Increase the lemon flavour by adding the zest and juice of ½ a lemon or 1 tablespoon bottled lemon juice instead of the splash of lemon juice.

APPLE AND CINNAMON LOAF CAKE

This recipe started off as muffins that I made at school many years ago, and eventually became a warm, sweet, moist loaf cake. It's quite soft due to the quantity of apples used, lending it a crumbly texture that makes it delicious to eat in a bowl with custard or natural yoghurt. It firms up by the next day – that is, if there's any left!

Serves 6

3 small apples, cored

zest and juice of ½ a lemon or 1 tablespoon bottled lemon juice

100g butter, plus extra to grease the tin

100g sugar

2 eggs

a generous handful of sultanas

180g self-raising flour (or 180g plain flour and 1 heaped teaspoon baking powder or bicarbonate of soda)

1 level teaspoon baking powder

a pinch of ground cinnamon

Preheat the oven to 180°C /350°F/gas 4 and lightly grease a small loaf tin. Line the tin with greaseproof paper.

Thinly slice the apples, grate the lemon zest over them followed by a squeeze of juice, and set to one side.

In a mixing bowl, cream the butter and sugar together until combined. Break the eggs into the bowl, tip in the lemony apples, and scatter in the sultanas. Mix quickly to make a soft, chunky mixture. Add the flour, baking powder and a shake of cinnamon, and stir well with a wooden spoon until smooth. Pour the cake batter into the greased tin and smooth the top using the spoon.

Bake for 40 to 45 minutes in the centre of the preheated oven until golden and springy – a sharp knife inserted into the middle should come out clean. When cooked, allow to cool for 10 minutes before turning out of the tin. Cut into slices and eat.

TIPS: Will keep in an airtight container or wrapped tightly in cling film for 3 to 4 days. It's delicious the next day when the cake settles and goes slightly gooey.

This mixture can also be used to make muffins – I never bother with muffin cases, just simply grease the individual cups in the tin and spoon 2 tablespoons of the mixture in. Bake for 15 to 20 minutes, until risen, golden and springy.

PEANUT BUTTER AND JAM THUMBPRINT COOKIES

Here I have brought together two of my favourite cookies into a classic combination of peanut butter and jam. My small boy loves making the thumbprints in these and spooning in the jam, and it's a happy rainy-day activity to do together – although having such tiny little thumbs, he does his with a teaspoon!

Makes 12 cookies

50g butter, plus extra to grease the baking sheet

2 tablespoons caster sugar

1 egg yolk

2 tablespoons crunchy peanut butter

8 tablespoons self-raising flour (or 8 tablespoons plain flour and 1 level teaspoon baking powder or bicarbonate of soda), plus extra to dust your hands

4 tablespoons jam

Preheat the oven to 180°C/350°F/gas 4, and lightly grease a baking sheet in preparation.

Cream the butter and sugar together in a mixing bowl with a wooden spoon until softened and well combined. Add the egg yolk and the peanut butter, and mix until the peanut butter is evenly distributed through the mixture. Spoon in the flour and stir to make a soft dough.

With lightly floured hands, break off a walnut-sized piece of dough. Place on the prepared baking sheet and flatten slightly with a fork. Repeat with the rest of the dough. Using your thumb, or a teaspoon, make a deep well in the centre of each flattened ball of dough – the cookies will flatten and spread out slightly as they cook, so don't be afraid to dig in!

Melt the jam slightly in a microwave for 30 seconds on a low setting, then spoon a little into the centre of each cookie.

Bake in the centre of the preheated oven for 10 to 12 minutes, or until golden.

TIPS: Try different flavour combinations, such as grated white chocolate in place of the peanut butter and lemon curd instead of jam. Or try dark chocolate with blackberry jam for a dark, delicious 'Black Forest gateau' version.

Serve the cookies warm from the oven with a scoop of frozen yoghurt – try making your own Peanut Butter and White Chocolate Frozen Yoghurt (see page 202).

PEANUT BUTTER AND WHITE CHOCOLATE FROZEN YOGHURT

This simple recipe is a must for any peanut butter lovers. Its first incarnation was as peanut butter-flavoured yoghurt – made by mixing two of my staple food items together for a sweet treat – and it went from there. I don't add sugar or syrup to sweeten this recipe when I make it as I like the slight tang of the peanut butter, but feel free to add a tablespoon or two if you wish.

Serves 4

500g natural yoghurt

200g crunchy peanut butter

100ml milk

optional: 2 tablespoons sugar (depending on how sweet the peanut butter is)

100g white chocolate

Pour the yoghurt into a mixing bowl and stir in the peanut butter and milk until well combined. Add the sugar, if using. Finely chop or grate the white chocolate and fold through. Put the whole bowl in the freezer for 1 hour, uncovered. Remove and stir well.

Line a 1lb loaf tin (approximately 17 x 7 x 6cm) with two or three layers of cling film, making sure to press it into the corners of the tin. Pour the semi-frozen mixture into the loaf tin, cover with more cling film and freeze for at least 4 hours.

Remove from the freezer and serve by the scoop, or tip out of the tin and serve in slices if preferred.

TIP: Replace the peanut butter with lemon curd for a sweet, zesty treat, or with 100g frozen berries. The flavour possibilities are endless …

BEERY BERRY CRUMBLE

This pudding came about a bit by accident, when I had the remains of a can of cheap bitter kicking about in the fridge door from the Beer and Sultana Bread (see page 30) and some frozen berries defrosted in a dish in the fridge that needed using up. Rather than drink half a flat beer and pick at squishy berries, I decided to make something out of them. And this, the result, is delicious. If you have brown sugar, do use it, as the deep treacly taste it brings is something else. If you don't, then white sugar will do just fine. Fresh berries can be expensive – look in the freezer department of the supermarket for a frozen mix for a fraction of the price! I've added apples to mine, but this is also delicious with plums to bulk it out instead. I will happily devour this crumble on its own, or served with cream, custard or ice cream – or straight from the dish when pretending to dish it up!

Serves 4

2 large apples

400g frozen or fresh berries

200ml bitter

100g sugar, plus 1 tablespoon for the berries

200g plain flour

100g butter (or 50g butter and 50g lard)

100g oats

Preheat the oven to 180°C/350°F/gas 4, and get out a deep ovenproof dish around 20cm in diameter to cook the crumble in.

Roughly chop the apples, discarding the cores, and toss into a medium-sized saucepan. Tip the berries into the pan, pour the bitter over the top, add the tablespoon of sugar and bring to the boil, watching carefully as beer can get a bit excitable when heated, depending on how old it is! Once the beer comes to the boil, reduce the pan to a medium simmer, and leave for 10 minutes to defrost the berries. If using fresh berries, simmer anyway to soften them.

Tip the flour and sugar into a large mixing bowl. Dice the butter – or butter and lard if using – into cubes and rub together with the flour and sugar until the mixture resembles fine breadcrumbs. Stir in the oats and set to one side.

Remove the beery berries and apples from the heat and using a slotted spoon transfer the fruit into the ovenproof dish. Starting from the outside edges to prevent soggy corners, spoon the crumble topping on to the berries evenly until it's all used up.

Pop the crumble into the preheated oven for 30 minutes, or until the top is golden and crisp. Allow to stand for a few minutes before serving, then eat.

TIP: The leftover beery berry juice works well as a sauce to serve with meat. Cook onions and a beef stock cube in it for a delicious gravy that goes well with sausages.

QUEEN OF HEARTS JAM TARTS

Jam tarts are one of those simple, delicious things that I remember consuming in droves in my childhood, but not so much as an adult. I always have flour in the cupboard and jam in the fridge, and this makes for a lovely rainy-day activity for small children to help with. Of course, you can cheat with jam tarts and buy some ready-to-roll shortcrust pastry, but where's the fun in that? Fill them with any jam you like or lemon curd, or to feed my peanut-butter-and-jam obsession I work a little peanut butter into the pastry mixture and fill with smooth strawberry jam.

Makes about 6 tarts, depending on the size of your cookie cutter

50g butter or 25g butter and 25g lard, plus extra to grease the muffin tray

120g plain flour, plus extra to knead the dough

1 tablespoon cold water

6 heaped teaspoons jam

Preheat the oven to 180°C/350°F/gas 4 and pop a tablespoon or wooden spoon into the freezer. Lightly grease a 6-cup muffin tray with a little butter or oil, and set to one side.

Chop the butter – or butter and lard – into small cubes and toss into a large mixing bowl. Add the flour and rub in with your fingertips until the mixture looks like fine breadcrumbs. If your hands start to become warm, rinse them under the cold tap.

Add a tablespoon of cold water to the floury 'breadcrumb' mixture, remove the spoon from the freezer and use it to mix the dough together.

Briefly knead the dough on a floured worktop and press or roll out until approximately 0.5cm thick. (I never, ever use a rolling pin, in fact I don't think I have one. I find that my palms work just fine.) Using a pastry cutter or a tea cup, cut circles from the pastry that are slightly bigger than the muffin cups.

One at a time, gently press a pastry circle into each cup of the muffin tray. Repeat until all the dough is used up. Pop a heaped teaspoon of jam into each pastry case – being careful to only fill two-thirds full, as the jam will bubble and spill out when cooked.

Bake in the centre of the preheated oven for 12 minutes, or until golden brown. Remove and allow to cool before serving.

TIP: These will keep in an airtight container for up to 3 days after baking. They also freeze beautifully – allow to cool, then freeze in a freezer bag or airtight container. Defrost in a microwave or oven on a low heat.

AND ANOTHER THING...

This section was born of the little extras that I put together from half a tin of this and that, or almost ropey old veggies at the back of the fridge.

Make a cooling raita from natural yoghurt to serve with curry (see page 213), a quick mint sauce from windowsill herbs and store cupboard basics (see page 212) or pickle eggs to snack on or pack in lunch boxes (see page 209).

As a nation, almost 4.2 million tonnes of the food we bought in 2012 ended up in the bin. But there's not much that you can't make into something else so, with a little guidance, here's how to turn those sad mushrooms at the back of the fridge into a haute cuisine ingredient for your store cupboard.

DRYING CHILLIES

I like to dry my home-grown chillies out and turn them into chilli flakes.

Preheat the oven to 180°C/350°F/gas 4. Snip the green stalks off the chillies, and lay them out whole on a baking tray. Pop the tray into the preheated oven for 20 minutes for the chillies to crisp up. The smaller ones take less time, so if you've got a mixture of sizes, check on the chillies after 10 to 15 minutes. When they crumble easily in your hand, they are good to go.

Take the dried chillies out of the oven, pop them into a bowl (or trusty tea cup), and chop into them with kitchen scissors. Be very careful of chilli dust flying around when you do this – chilli dust up your nose is not nice! Pour the chilli flakes into a spice jar and seal with a lid.

DRYING MUSHROOMS

Before your mushrooms go slimy in the back of the fridge, dry them out to store them. Dried mushrooms are marketed as a gourmet ingredient when, really, they're very simple to make. I keep my eyes peeled for mushrooms on special offer, or in the reduced chiller at the supermarket, and stock up on them to dry out at home.

Preheat the oven to 180°C/350°F/gas 4. Clean any dirt from your mushrooms with a dry tea towel or dish cloth, with paper towel or – as I do – use a clean soft toothbrush. Slice or chop the mushrooms as desired. Chopping them into smallish pieces means that they will dry quicker, but slices look nice – it's up to you.

Lay the prepared mushrooms on a baking tray and put into the preheated oven for 45 minutes,

turning halfway through. Alternatively, if you don't want to use the oven, cover the baking tray with a clean tea towel and leave it on the side in the kitchen for 2 days (away from any curious pets!) Remove, cool and transfer the dried mushrooms to a clean jar or airtight container.

TIP: *Dried mushrooms have a stronger flavour than fresh mushrooms, so a few will go a long way Add them to soups, stocks, casseroles and risottos to reconstitute – the mushrooms will plump back up when they have absorbed some liquid.*

EGGS

The older an egg is, the larger the pores in the shell become – but this is not always obvious at a glance. To check if an egg is safe to use, pop it into a glass of cold water. If it is fresh, it will sink. If it is old, it will float.

Pickled eggs

My favourite method of storing eggs is to hard boil them then pickle them in a jar. When I was a teenager, my dad and I used to have pickled eggs from the chip shop and dip them in thick, spicy curry sauce. Pickled eggs make great snacks, for busy hungry people and Small Boys alike.

6 eggs
white wine vinegar, to cover
1 teaspoon salt

Hard boil the eggs in a saucepan of water for 6 minutes. Remove from the heat, drain and allow to cool before carefully peeling off the shells. Pop the peeled eggs into a large clean jar with an airtight lid, cover completely with the wine vinegar and add the salt. Seal the jar and shake gently to dissolve the salt. The eggs will keep for a few months as long as they remain covered in the pickling liquid, but once the jar has been opened, store in the fridge.

FREEZING VEG

If you have too much of any vegetables and you won't use them all before they're past their best, don't despair – freeze them instead. Prepared this way, veg will keep for up to 3 months. The best way to freeze vegetables is to blanch them first.

First, put a saucepan of water on to boil and fill a second saucepan with cold water – possibly even put some ice cubes in there.

Peel or clean (vigorously rinse or gently wipe, depending on what veg you've got) and then chop your vegetables. I like to trim green beans, slice mushrooms, carrots or parsnips, dice onions and potatoes, and chop cauliflower or broccoli into little trees – but how you chop your veg is up to you!

Pop a large spoonful of prepared vegetables into the pan of boiling water, slowly count to ten and remove the veg with a slotted spoon straight into the pan of cold water to cool down. Repeat until everything has been blanched. Drain the cold vegetables, then transfer to an airtight container or freezer bag and pop into the freezer.

GARLIC

Garlic is often cheaper to buy in bulk packs than as individual bulbs – so every now and again I buy a bag or two containing 10 bulbs and spend an hour preserving them. There are three main methods I like to use: freezing, making garlic paste and preserving in vinegar.

Freezing

Break open the garlic bulb to remove the cloves, and for each clove chop off the ends and peel away the papery skin. You can freeze the garlic cloves whole if you want to use them whole, but I finely chop mine and freeze the chopped garlic spread out thinly (for ease of breaking off a chunk when it's frozen). You can just pop the frozen chopped garlic straight into the dish when cooking.

Garlic paste

Garlic paste must be stored frozen, as homemade garlic paste can cause botulism (due to the low acidity of the garlic, the lack of oxygen in the oil and the warm room-temperature conditions). Commercially made garlic paste is made in sterile conditions with added preservatives and so doesn't need to be frozen. Homemade garlic paste is easy to use – freeze it in ice cube trays and then scoop a cube out to use in cooking. You can add chilli, lemon or herbs to create different flavours.

1 bulb of garlic
oil
optional: additional flavourings, such as chopped fresh chilli, lemon zest or dried herbs

Break open the garlic bulb to remove the cloves, and for each clove chop off the ends and peel away the papery skin. Put the peeled garlic cloves into a blender and cover with oil, then blend until the cloves have been completely mixed into the oil. Add any additional flavouring you want to use and blend again. Pour the garlic paste into ice cube trays or small airtight containers and freeze.

Preserving in vinegar

This is the easiest method for preserving garlic, with no chopping or blending required. These preserved cloves will keep in the fridge, sealed in the jar, for up to 3 months. When all the garlic has been used up, use the leftover garlicky vinegar, mixed with an equal amount of oil, as a delicious dressing for salad or green vegetables.

1 bulb of garlic
red or white wine vinegar
1 level teaspoon salt

Break open the garlic bulb to remove the cloves, and for each clove chop off the ends and peel away the papery skin. Place the peeled cloves in a small clean dry jam jar with a lid. Pour over enough wine vinegar to cover, add the salt, screw on the lid and shake to distribute.

LEFTOVER BREAD

Ever noticed that home-made bread tends to go stale quite quickly, and shop-bought bread tends to go mouldy? Well, to avoid wasting your bread, but if it's beyond the 'bung it in the freezer' stage of freshness, why not make croutons or breadcrumbs. Croutons can be popped into a large warming bowl of soup – try the Really Tomatoey Basilly Soup (see page 44) – for a crunchy treat, and breadcrumbs are delicious tossed on top of a pasta dish or used for dressing a fillet of fish.

To make croutons

Preheat the oven to 180°C/350°F/gas 4. Cut leftover bread into cubes, as large or as small as you like. I make my croutons fairly hefty – around 2.5cm on each side. Pop the bread cubes on to a very lightly greased baking tray and cook for 5 minutes in the centre of the preheated oven.

To make breadcrumbs

Slice up leftover bread and lightly toast the slices on both sides. Place in a freezer bag, tie securely and roll a rolling pin (or wine bottle or equivalent) repeatedly over the bag to break up the toasted bread inside into breadcrumbs. Alternatively, if you have a blender, tear the lightly toasted bread into small pieces and whizz in the blender for a few minutes.

TIP: *Breadcrumbs and croutons can both be stored in the freezer until required. Experiment with different flavours of breadcrumbs – you can add dried herbs, zest from citrus fruits, chilli flakes or black pepper.*

LEFTOVER WINE

Leftover wine? What's leftover wine? Well, it happens occasionally. I use wine a lot in my cooking – even the cheapest bottle of plonk can transform rice and mushrooms into a delicious risotto. Some supermarkets sell small bottles of cooking wine, which is a bonus as it doesn't feel as extravagant as spending on a larger bottle in one go – although that 750ml bottle will last for a good few casseroles and risottos, plus swigs in between!

Keep leftover white wine in the fridge, with the lid screwed back on it or a teaspoon in the neck if it was a bottle with a cork. (I'm not sure if the teaspoon trick is just an old wives' tale, but we used to do it at the pub I worked in, and the wine always tasted good to me.)

Freeze leftover red wine in ice cube trays until required. Wine doesn't completely freeze, though, so only fill the tray two-thirds full and put it inside a freezer bag or wrap the tray in cling film when frozen, to prevent it making a mess in your freezer. If you have a freezer with a fancy compartment specifically for ice cubes, pop it in there.

TIP: *Mix one part vinegar to four parts wine and leave for several weeks to do its thing. Combine with a little oil for a delicious dressing for a bean salad, or add it to the onions when cooking a risotto, then allow them to cook for slightly longer to get rid of the tanginess.*

LOVELY LAVENDER

I can highly recommend having a small lavender plant as part of a windowsill herb garden or, if you have any outdoor space, plant one outside and watch it grow and grow. I use the tiny fragrant flowers in biscuits, scones, cakes, sweet oil or to flavour sugar for herbal tea. You can enliven the cheapest tub of vanilla ice cream with them.

Dried lavender

Pick as much lavender as you have or can find. Rinse under a cold running tap in a mesh sieve and pat dry with a tea towel.

Line a baking tray with either a clean dry tea towel, baking parchment or greaseproof paper.

Break up the heads to separate the buds and flowers from the green stalky plant. Place the flowers and buds on the baking tray.

Leave for 3 days to dry out completely, then tip into an airtight container. Seal and store – the dried lavender will keep for months.

Lavender sugar

Use as a sprinkle on cakes or when icing biscuits with a little lemon juice and zest, or add 1 teaspoon to a mug of chamomile tea to help you sleep at night.

250g brown or white sugar
6 heads of dried lavender

Pour the sugar into an airtight container, such as an old clean jam jar. Pick the flowers and buds off the lavender heads one by one and drop into the sugar. Seal the container and shake gently to distribute the lavender throughout the sugar. Leave for a few days for the flavour to infuse.

Lavender and herb salt

200g salt (preferably sea salt)
2 heads of dried lavender
1 tablespoon finely chopped fresh rosemary or thyme

Put the salt into an airtight container. Sea salt is best, but ordinary table salt will do just fine. Then put in the flowers and buds from the lavender heads, add the chopped herbs and seal the container. Shake gently to distribute the flavourings and leave for a few days to infuse.

QUICK MINT SAUCE

If you grow your own mint, or have any left over from a bunch used in another recipe, here's a very good use for it. Once you know how to make your own mint sauce, you'll never buy it from the supermarket again. You just need a clean jar with an airtight screwtop lid. To chop it, I pop my mint into a large mug, stalks included, and chop chop chop with kitchen scissors until it's in small, fine pieces! This is best made a day ahead to allow the flavours to develop.

2 large handfuls of fresh mint
a pinch of salt
2 tablespoons sugar
6 tablespoons boiling water
6 tablespoons white wine vinegar

Finely chop the mint, stalks included, into a mug or bowl, then scrape into the jar that you will be storing the sauce in. Add the salt, sugar and boiling water. Screw the lid on tight, and shake to combine. Unscrew the lid and leave to cool.

When cooled, add the vinegar, stir and put the lid back on again. Pop into the fridge and use as required.

QUICK APPLE SAUCE

A swift and delicious accompaniment to my beloved bacon, or any other pork dish, this apple sauce also works well with leftover chicken or turkey in a sandwich or pitta bread. No exact quantities are given for this recipe as it depends on how many apples you have and how large they are, but allow about a tablespoon of cider or a teaspoon of cider vinegar per apple as a rule of thumb.

oil, to grease the baking tray
fresh thyme, to taste
(2 sprigs per 6 apples)

*cider (1 tablespoon
per apple) or cider vinegar
(1 teaspoon per apple)
a shake of black pepper
apples*

Preheat your oven to 180°C/350°F/gas 4 and lightly grease a baking tray or roasting dish.

Finely chop the thyme – I do mine in a teacup with kitchen scissors – and add the cider or cider vinegar and pepper.

Do not peel the apples. Quarter them, and carefully cut out the hard core from each piece. Put into a mixing bowl and pour the cidery-thyme liquid on top. Toss gently to coat the apples. Place the apples skin side up on the baking tray or roasting dish, and cover with foil. Bake in the centre of the preheated oven for 30 minutes, or until the apples are mushy and soft.

Remove from the oven, allow to cool for a few minutes (until they are cool enough to handle) and scrape the flesh from the skins into a bowl. Add any juices from the tray that they have been cooking in. Mash with a fork or purée with a hand blender.

This apple sauce can be stored in a sealed jar in the fridge for 3 days, or frozen in an ice cube tray for future use.

RAITA

Raita is an Indian sauce or dip, often made with yoghurt, to accompany hot or spicy dishes. I make a simple raita to pour over Small Boy's curry. The three versions given below can be made from standard store cupboard and fresh ingredients used throughout this book. Once you have the hang of it, experiment with fresh coriander, ground cumin, ground turmeric, garlic, onion, chilli – the possibilities are endless!

Peanut raita

*100g peanut butter, softened
100ml natural yoghurt
optional: a pinch of dried chilli flakes or
½ a red chilli, chopped
fresh chopped coriander, to garnish*

Mix together the peanut butter and yoghurt in a small bowl. Stir in the chilli flakes or chopped chilli, if using, and sprinkle over the fresh chopped coriander.

Potato raita

*250g fresh potatoes or ½ a 550g tin of potatoes
a shake of ground cumin
1 red chilli, chopped
2 tablespoons natural yoghurt*

If using fresh potatoes, wash them, then dice and boil in a saucepan for about 20 minutes until soft. Or, if using tinned potatoes, simply drain. Put the potatoes in a bowl, pour in 120ml water and mash together. Add the cumin, chilli and natural yoghurt, and stir through. Serve warm or cold.

Mint raita

*½ a cucumber or courgette
a handful of fresh mint
200ml natural yoghurt*

Grate the cucumber or courgette on to kitchen paper to absorb the excess water. Finely chop the mint into a bowl and mix in the yoghurt. Squeeze the grated veg to get rid of as much water as possible and mix into the yoghurt as well.

HUNGER HURTS – ONE YEAR LATER

An excerpt from my blog in July 2013:

The original blog post 'Hunger Hurts' was my turning point – the rock bottom that I hit, the night I decided to hold a big open-house sale and sell everything that I could to raise enough money to clear my rent arrears. It's the night I resigned myself to sacrificing everything I had in the way of material possessions, in order to keep four walls around me. I cannot read those words myself without my stomach twisting, as I remember the cold bloody winter sitting in a flat with no heating, the Christmas Day spent by myself because I realized my son would have a better time at his father's than in a freezing cold flat with no tree and no presents – as I lay on my sofa without him and sobbed, alone.

'Hunger Hurts' is the most-read post on my blog to date and is still relevant today, when half a million people are reported to rely on food banks here in the seventh-richest country in the world. I urge you to read it and reread it until you can comprehend what life is like for those half a million people – and those many, many more who do not receive the help that they so desperately need.

The timeline of events over the last year or so has been a rollercoaster. Xanthe Clay from the Telegraph came over in February 2013 to have Moroccan Not-a-Tagine for lunch and wrote her article 'My 49p Lunch with a Girl Called Jack'. This in turn led to a recipe book deal with Penguin and subsequent appearances on Sky News, the BBC and ITV to talk about food and poverty. The Guardian described me in July as 'the face of modern poverty' – and indeed I have been to the G8 summit and spoken in Parliament on poverty issues. With that comes a public backlash, with hurtful comments about my weight, my appearance, my sexuality, my former landlord's choice of decor, my parenting – as some people forget I am a person and that I hurt, and I feel, and I cry, too.

And for those that regularly ask me – yes, I still spend around £10 a week on my food shop. I'm learning to indulge again, but indulgence for me these days is a jar of black olives or some (value range) salted cashews. I think once you learn how to eat great food on a low budget, it's impossible to go back to spending £50 a week on food again.

Although my circumstances have changed somewhat in the past year – I have a job, I'm self-employed and I have a recipe book deal – I cannot put down the mantle and stop campaigning nor forget where I have come from. I am an ambassador for Child Poverty Action Group and I have raised over £6,000 for charity through two extremely personal challenges: sleeping rough in a car park for the YMCA in March and Living Below the Line for Oxfam in June.

Regular readers will be able to recite the closing sentence of 'Hunger Hurts', which is as true today for half a million people in the UK as it was for me then on 30 July 2012, typing through angry tears that poverty isn't just having no heating, or not quite enough food, or unplugging your fridge and turning your hot water off. Poverty is the sinking feeling when your small boy finishes his one Weetabix and says, 'More, Mummy? Bread and jam please, Mummy?' as you're wondering whether to take the TV or the guitar to the pawn shop first, and how to tell him that there is no bread or jam.

For those asking, 'What can I do to help?' – well, donate something to your local food bank: tins, nappies, baby formula, UHT milk, cereals, toiletries, pasta, rice, tinned fruit and vegetables. Volunteer at a children's centre or a playgroup – I found those free activities with Small Boy were literally a lifeline to me when I had nothing to do in my day, no money, nothing to look forward to. Visit your local volunteer centre and see how you can help. Donate old clothes, shoes and blankets to your local homeless shelter. Don't step over people in the street – give them the £3 you might have spent on a latte.

I almost have my happy ending. Almost. But hundreds of thousands of families in Britain are starving and they don't get a book deal, and they don't get to sit on the Sky News sofa and shout at politicians about how it is. So until 'Hunger Hurts' becomes an antiquated, Dickensian fable of what life WAS like in quaintly titled 'Austerity Britain', while 'Hunger Hurts' is still true for just ONE family, let alone half a million people, while those like Lord Freud can get away with pontificating on the 'unnecessary' nature of food banks, I must carry on raging against the machine, shouting at the rain, meeting with government advisers and repeating again and again and again and again until they get it.

Half a million people in the UK are relying on food handouts. Food banks are not the answer; they are a sticking plaster. There comes a time when you need to stop just pulling people out of the river. You need to go upstream, and find out why they're falling in.

Index

Page references in **bold** are for photographs.

Entries in **large bold** are for 'hero ingredients', things to base a dish around. When planning meals I open my cupboard and see what's there, and what I can make from it. By cooking around what you have, or using similar ingredients through the week, you can make a great number of recipes, as listed below each one.

A

anchovies:

battered anchovies with quick tarty sauce **148**, 149

savoury tomato sauce 83

apples:

apple and cinnamon loaf cake 198, **199**

beery berry crumble **204**, 205

honey and mustard glazed gammon joint with apple sauce 170, 171

quick apple sauce 212–13

aubergines:

baba ghanoush 122, **123**

Keralan aubergine curry 126, **127**

melitzanosalata 126

not meatballs **120**, 121

avgolemono **56**, 57

B

baba ghanoush 122, **123**

bacon: 168

best macaroni with bacon and spinach 182

Brie and bacon risotto 102, **103**

car-Brie-nara **90**, 91

ham, pea and mint casserole 180, **181**

mushroom, bacon and ale casserole 183

oh my God dinner 175

sausage and lentil one-pot dinner 186

spring piggy 176, **177**

warm chickpea salad with bacon and olives 65

baked beans:

mixed bean goulash 66, **67**

Mumma Jack's best-ever chilli 70

turkey meatballs **158**, 159

bananas:

banana sultana pancakes 31

vegan banana bread 31

basil:

best-o pesto 84

really tomatoey basilly soup 44

Roman pasta with mandarins and a creamy basil sauce **96**, 97

battered anchovies with quick tarty sauce **148**, 149

beans:

carrot, cumin and kidney bean burgers **62**, 63

carrot, cumin and kidney bean soup 47

creamy Greek cheese and courgette pasta 98

gigantes plaki **72**, 73

Mexican chocolate, chilli and black bean soup 52, **53**

mixed bean goulash 66, **67**

Mumma Jack's best-ever chilli 70

oh my God dinner 175

pork and beans cassoulet 174

Sicilian-style sardines with pasta and green beans 152, **153**

sort-of paella **110**, 111

spring piggy 176, **177**

tomato and haricot bean soup 45

turkey meatballs **158**, 159

vegetable masala curry 119

winter pasta alla Genovese 94, **95**

see also chickpeas; lentils

beer:

beer and sultana bread 30

beery berry crumble **204**, 205

mushroom, bacon and ale casserole 183

sausage and beer casserole **178**, 179

berries:

beery berry crumble **204**, 205

biscuits: peanut butter and jam thumbprint cookies **200**, 201

black beans:

Mexican chocolate, chilli and black bean soup 52, **53**

bread:

beer and sultana bread 30

breadcrumbs 211

chickpea and tomato best brunch loaf **26**, 27

courgette, sultana and lemon bread **32**, 33

crackerbread 24

croutons 211

fishy cakes 142

garlic, herb and lemon bread 35

leftover 211

mandarin and poppy seed loaf 34

panzanella **134**, 135

soda bread **22**, 23

sunshine bread 25

vegan banana bread 31

white chocolate tea bread **38**, 39

Brie:

Brie and bacon risotto 102, **103**

car-Brie-nara **90**, 91

courgette, tomato and Brie gratin 108, **109**

oh my God dinner 175

onion, cabbage and cheese pasta 93

bubbles and squeaks 118

burgers:

carrot, cumin and kidney bean burgers **62**, 63

smoky red lentil burgers 76

butter beans:
    gigantes plaki **72**, 73

C

cabbage:

bubbles and squeaks 118

cabbage griddle scones 28, **29**

colcannon 136

onion, cabbage and cheese pasta 93

spring piggy 176, **177**

car-Brie-nara **90**, 91

carrots:

carrot and coriander soup 46

carrot, cumin and kidney bean burgers **62**, 63

carrot, cumin and kidney bean soup 47

carrot ribbon pasta 89

chickpea, carrot and coriander falafels **68**, 69

creamy mustard chicken with winter veg 162, **163**

love soup 42, **43**

Moroccan not-a-tagine 130, **131**

spiced lentil soup 58

vegetable masala curry 119

cassoulet: pork and beans cassoulet 174

cheese: **14**

penny pizzas 36, **37**

see also Brie; feta

chestnuts:

chestnut and red wine casserole **128**, 129

chicken: **156**

chicken chasseur 160

creamy mustard chicken with winter veg 162, **163**

Diet-Coke chicken 166, **167**

easy chicken satay 161

Spanish-style chicken **164**, 165

chickpeas:

chickpea, carrot and coriander falafels **68**, 69

chickpea and tomato best brunch loaf **26**, 27

hummus **78**, 79

peach and chickpea curry 74, **75**

warm chickpea salad with bacon and olives 65

chillies:

creamy salmon pasta with a chilli lemon kick 144, **145**

drying chillies 209

feisty soup 49

firecracker sausages with tragedy mash **184**, 185

Keralan aubergine curry 126, **127**

Mexican chocolate, chilli and black bean soup 52, **53**

Mumma Jack's best-ever chilli 70

chocolate: **14**

chocolate buttons 193

Mexican chocolate, chilli and black bean soup 52, **53**

Mumma Jack's best-ever chilli 70

my cakeys 192

peanut butter and white chocolate frozen yoghurt 202, **203**

white chocolate and peach traybake **190**, 191

white chocolate tea bread **38**, 39

cinnamon:

apple and cinnamon loaf cake 198, **199**

cockles:

spaghetti with cockles 147

cola:

Diet-Coke chicken 166, **167**

colcannon 136

cookies: peanut butter and jam thumbprint cookies **200**, 201

coriander:

carrot and coriander soup 46

chickpea, carrot and coriander falafels **68**, 69

cornflakes:

my cakeys 192

courgettes:

courgette and mint fritters 116, **117**

courgette, sultana and lemon bread **32**, 33

courgette, tomato and Brie gratin 108, **109**

creamy Greek cheese and courgette pasta 98

mint raita 213

oh my God dinner 175

potato salad with Greek cheese, courgette and yoghurt 133

roasted courgette and mint soup 50

summer pasta alla Genovese 94, **95**

crackerbread 24

croutons 211

crumble: beery berry crumble **204**, 205

cumin:

carrot, cumin and kidney bean burgers **62**, 63

carrot, cumin and kidney bean soup 47

curry:

Keralan aubergine curry 126, **127**

peach and chickpea curry 74, **75**

vegetable masala curry 119

D

daal: warm spicy daal 77

E

eggs:

avgolemono **56**, 57

pickled 209

F

feisty soup 49

feta:

creamy Greek cheese and courgette pasta 98

gigantes plaki **72**, 73

melitzanosalata 126

potato salad with Greek cheese, courgette and yoghurt 133

simple prawns with feta and tomatoes 142

firecracker sausages with tragedy mash **184**, 185

fish paste:

  creamy salmon pasta with a chilli lemon kick 144, **145**

fish pie **140**, 141

fishy cakes 142

flour: 14, 15

  apple and cinnamon loaf cake 198, **199**

  beer and sultana bread 30

  beery berry crumble **204**, 205

  cabbage griddle scones 28, **29**

  chickpea and tomato best brunch loaf **26**, 27

  courgette, sultana and lemon bread **32**, 33

  crackerbread 24

  garlic, herb and lemon bread 35

  gnocchi **114**, 115

  mandarin and poppy seed loaf 34

  Paddington Bear sponge puddings **196**, 197

  peanut butter and jam thumbprint cookies **200**, 201

  penny pizzas 36, **37**

  queen of hearts jam tarts 206, 207

  school dinner days jam Swiss roll 194, **195**

  soda bread **22**, 23

  sunshine bread 25

  vegan banana bread 31

  white chocolate and peach traybake **190**, 191

  white chocolate tea bread **38**, 39

fritters: courgette and mint fritters 116, **117**

fruit 14

  see also *individual fruits*

G

gammon:

  honey and mustard glazed gammon joint with apple sauce **170**, 171

garlic:

  feisty soup 49

  freezing 210

  garlic, herb and lemon bread 35

  garlic and parsley risotto 104

  garlic paste 210

  preserving in vinegar 210–11

gigantes plaki **72**, 73

ginger:

  feisty soup 49

  love soup 42, **43**

gnocchi **114**, 115

goulash: mixed bean goulash 66, **67**

green beans:

  creamy Greek cheese and courgette pasta 98

  oh my God dinner 175

  Sicilian-style sardines with pasta and green beans 152, **153**

  sort-of paella **110**, 111

  spring piggy 176, **177**

  vegetable masala curry 119

  winter pasta alla Genovese 94, **95**

griddle scones 28, **29**

H

haddock:

  Jack's simple fish pie **140**, 141

haggis-style meatballs 187

ham:

  ham, pea and mint casserole 180, **181**

haricot beans:

  mixed bean goulash 66, **67**

  Mumma Jack's best-ever chilli 70

  pork and beans cassoulet 174

  tomato and haricot bean soup 45

  turkey meatballs **158**, 159

herbs: 16

  lavender and herb salt 212

  see also individual herbs

herring roes:

  scampi roes 150, **151**

hummus **78**, 79

J

jam:

  peanut butter and jam thumbprint cookies **200**, 201

  queen of hearts jam tarts 206, **207**

  school dinner days jam Swiss roll 194, *195*

K

Keralan aubergine curry 126, **127**

kidney beans:

  carrot, cumin and kidney bean burgers **62**, 63

  carrot, cumin and kidney bean soup 47

  mixed bean goulash 66, **67**

  Mumma Jack's best-ever chilli 70

L

lavender: 211

  chocolate buttons 193

  dried 212

  lavender and herb salt 212

  lavender sugar 212

lemon: 14

  avgolemono **56**, 57

  courgette, sultana and lemon bread **32**, 33

  creamy salmon pasta with a chilli lemon kick 144, **145**

  feisty soup 49

  garlic, herb and lemon bread 35

  oven-baked fish in best tomato sauce with lemon and parsley rice **154**, 155

lentils:

  lemony spinach pasta with brown lentils 92

lentil Bolognese 64

sausage and lentil one-pot dinner 186

smoky red lentil burgers 76

spiced lentil soup 58

warm spicy daal 77

love soup 42, **43**

M

macaroni:

best macaroni with bacon and spinach 182

macaroni peas 99

mandarins:

mandarin and poppy seed loaf 34

Roman pasta with mandarins and a creamy basil sauce **96**, 97

Spanish-style chicken **164**, 165

marmalade:

firecracker sausages with tragedy mash **184**, 185

Paddington Bear sponge puddings **196**, 197

masala: vegetable masala curry 119

meatballs:

haggis-style meatballs 187

not meatballs **120**, 121

turkey meatballs **158**, 159

melitzanosalata 126

Mexican chocolate, chilli and black bean soup 52, **53**

mint:

courgette and mint fritters 116, **117**

creamy Greek cheese and courgette pasta 98

ham, pea and mint casserole 180, **181**

mint raita 213

pea and mint risotto 105

quick mint sauce 212

roasted courgette and mint soup 50

summer pasta alla Genovese 94, **95**

Moroccan not-a-tagine 130, **131**

Mumma Jack's best-ever chilli 70

mushrooms:

chestnut and red wine casserole **128**, 129

chicken chasseur 160

drying 209

earthy red wine and mushroom risotto **106**, 107

mushroom, bacon and ale casserole 183

mushroom chasseur **124**, 125

mushroom and spinach pasta 88

mushroom stroganoff 132

red wine and mushroom soup 51

sausage and beer casserole **178**, 179

mushy pea soup 59

mustard:

honey and mustard glazed gammon joint with apple sauce **170**, 171

O

oh my God dinner 175

oil 14

olives:

warm chickpea salad with bacon and olives 65

onions:

bubbles and squeaks 118

love soup 42, **43**

onion, cabbage and cheese pasta 93

onion pasta with parsley and red wine **86**, 87

onion soup with red wine 55

oranges: *see mandarins*

P

Paddington Bear sponge puddings **196**, 197

paella **110**, 111

panzanella **134**, 135

paprika:

Spanish-style chicken **164**, 165

parsley:

best-o pesto 84

garlic, herb and lemon bread 35

garlic and parsley risotto 104

onion pasta with parsley and red wine **86**, 87

oven-baked fish in best tomato sauce with lemon and parsley rice **154**, 155

pasta: 14, 80

best macaroni with bacon and spinach 182

best-o pesto 84

car-Brie-nara **90**, 91

carrot ribbon pasta 89

creamy Greek cheese and courgette pasta 98

creamy salmon pasta with a chilli lemon kick 144, **145**

easy salmon pasta 146

lemony spinach pasta with brown lentils 92

lentil Bolognese 64

macaroni peas 99

mushroom and spinach pasta 88

oh my God dinner 175

onion, cabbage and cheese pasta 93

onion pasta with parsley and red wine **86**, 87

Roman pasta with mandarins and a creamy basil sauce **96**, 97

Sicilian-style sardines with pasta and green beans 152, **153**

spaghetti with cockles 147

summer pasta alla Genovese 94, **95**

use-me-for-anything tomato sauce **82**, 83

peaches:

peach and chickpea curry 74, **75**

white chocolate and peach traybake **190**, 191

peanut butter:

easy chicken satay 161

my cakeys 192

peanut butter and jam thumbprint cookies **200**, 201

peanut butter and white chocolate frozen yoghurt 202, **203**

peanut raita 213

peas:

ham, pea and mint casserole 180, **181**

macaroni peas 99

mushy pea soup 59

pea and mint risotto 105

sort-of paella **110**, 111

summer pasta alla Genovese 94, **95**

penny pizzas 36, **37**

pesto:

best-o pesto 84

summer pasta alla Genovese 94, **95**

pilchards

fishy cakes 142

see also sardines

pineapple:

sunshine bread 25

pizza 36, **37**

poppy seeds:

mandarin and poppy seed loaf 34

pork:

haggis-style meatballs 187

pork kokkinisto 172, **173**

see also *bacon*; *gammon*; *ham*; *sausages*

potatoes:

bubbles and squeaks 118

colcannon 136

firecracker sausages with tragedy mash **184**, 185

fishy cakes 142

gnocchi **114**, 115

ham, pea and mint casserole 180, **181**

Jack's simple fish pie **140**, 141

Moroccan not-a-tagine 130, **131**

potato raita 213

potato salad with Greek cheese, courgette and yoghurt 133

saag aloo 137

sausage and lentil one-pot dinner 186

simple spiced potato soup 54

vegetable masala curry 119

summer pasta alla Genovese 94, **95**

prawns:

simple prawns with feta and tomatoes 142

sort-of paella **110**, 111

prunes:

Moroccan not-a-tagine 130, **131**

pulses *see chickpeas; lentils*

Q

queen of hearts jam tarts 206, **207**

R

raita 213

red kidney beans *see kidney beans*

rice: 14, 100

avgolemono **56**, 57

Brie and bacon risotto 102, **103**

courgette, tomato and Brie gratin 108, **109**

earthy red wine and mushroom risotto **106**, 107

garlic and parsley risotto 104

oven-baked fish in best tomato sauce with lemon and parsley rice **154**, 155

pea and mint risotto 105

sort-of paella **110**, 111

roasted courgette and mint soup 50

Roman pasta with mandarins and a creamy basil sauce **96**, 97

S

saag aloo 137

salmon:

creamy salmon pasta with a chilli lemon kick 144, **145**

easy salmon pasta 146

sardines:

Sicilian-style sardines with pasta and green beans 152, **153**

see also pilchards

satay:

easy chicken satay 161

sausages:

firecracker sausages with tragedy mash **184**, 185

pork and beans cassoulet 174

sausage and beer casserole **178**, 179

sausage and lentil one-pot dinner 186

scampi roes 150, **151**

school dinner days jam Swiss roll 194, **195**

scones: cabbage griddle scones 28, **29**

Sicilian-style sardines with pasta and green beans 152, **153**

soda bread **22**, 23

spaghetti:

oh my God dinner 175

spaghetti with cockles 147

Spanish-style chicken **164**, 165

spiced lentil soup 58

spiced potato soup 54

spices 15

see also *individual spices*

spinach:

best macaroni with bacon and spinach 182

Jack's simple fish pie **140**, 141

lemony spinach pasta with brown lentils 92

mushroom and spinach pasta 88

saag aloo 137

vegetable masala curry 119

sponge puddings **196**, 197

spring piggy 176, **177**

stroganoff: mushroom stroganoff 132

sultanas:

apple and cinnamon loaf cake 198, **199**

banana sultana pancakes 31

beer and sultana bread 30

courgette, sultana and lemon bread **32**, 33

vegan banana bread 31

sunshine bread 25

sweet potatoes:

firecracker sausages with tragedy mash **184**, 185

Swiss roll 194, **195**

T

tagine 130, **131**

tea:

white chocolate tea bread 38, 39

tomatoes:

baba ghanoush 122, **123**

chestnut and red wine casserole **128**, 129

chicken chasseur 160

chickpea and tomato best brunch loaf **26**, 27

courgette, tomato and Brie gratin 108, **109**

Diet-Coke chicken 166, **167**

feisty soup 49

gigantes plaki **72**, 73

Keralan aubergine curry 126, **127**

lentil Bolognese 64

Mexican chocolate, chilli and black bean soup 52, **53**

Moroccan not-a-tagine 130, **131**

Mumma Jack's best-ever chilli 70

mushroom chasseur **124**, 125

oven-baked fish in best tomato sauce with lemon and parsley rice **154**, 155

panzanella **134**, 135

peach and chickpea curry 74, **75**

penny pizzas 36, **37**

pork and beans cassoulet 174

pork kokkinisto 172, **173**

really tomatoey basilly soup 44

sausage and beer casserole **178**, 179

sausage and lentil one-pot dinner 186

simple prawns with feta and tomatoes 142

sort-of paella **110**, 111

spaghetti with cockles 147

Spanish-style chicken **164**, 165

spiced lentil soup 58

tomato and haricot bean soup 45

use-me-for-anything tomato sauce **82**, 83

vegetable masala curry 119

warm spicy daal 77

turkey: 156

turkey meatballs **158**, 159

V

vegan banana bread 31

vegetables 15, 112

freezing 210

vegetable masala curry 119

see also individual vegetables

W

warm spicy daal 77

white chocolate tea bread **38**, 39

wine: 15

chestnut and red wine casserole **128**, 129

chicken chasseur 160

earthy red wine and mushroom risotto **106**, 107

leftover 211

mushroom chasseur **124**, 125

onion pasta with parsley and red wine **86**, 87

onion soup with red wine 55

pork kokkinisto 172, **173**

red wine and mushroom soup 51

Y

yoghurt: 14

battered anchovies with quick tarty sauce **148**, 149

car-Brie-nara **90**, 91

creamy Greek cheese and courgette pasta 98

creamy mustard chicken with winter veg 162, **163**

creamy salmon pasta with a chilli lemon kick 144, **145**

easy chicken satay 161

mushroom stroganoff 132

mushy pea soup 59

peanut butter and white chocolate frozen yoghurt 202, **203**

potato salad with Greek cheese, courgette and yoghurt 133

raita 213

Roman pasta with mandarins and a creamy basil sauce **96**, 97

school dinner days jam Swiss roll 194, **195**

simple spiced potato soup 54

vegetable masala curry 119

Acknowledgements

Where to start with these?

FIRSTLY, THANK YOU FOR BUYING A COPY OF THIS BOOK, you person with clearly excellent taste in books. I hope you find it extremely useful.

THANK YOU TO MS FARQUHAR, the best Home Economics teacher ever, and MISS SAVILLE (yes, I know you're married now, but you'll always be Miss Saville to me); to ESME KADIC, for praising my rock cake recipe when I was fourteen and put ten times as much sugar in them by accident, and SHEILA, for the gentle support through my GCSE.

THANK YOU TO MY DARLING SON, who eats almost everything I put in front of him, and who dragged me out of the black hole with his three-year-old tenacity and that need to carry on.

THANK YOU TO XANTHE CLAY, who accidentally catapulted me to fame in February 2013 with a charming account in the *Telegraph* of my Moroccan cooking and her description of my 'fierce competency', then held my hand through the Fortnum & Mason award when I thought I was going to fall over in shock. Thank you to Fiona Beckett, Tom Parker-Bowles and Dan Saladino for being sounding boards, foodie friends and generally lovely.

THANK YOU TO PATRICK BUTLER at the *Guardian*, ROS WYNNE-JONES at the *Mirror* and PAMELA OWEN at the *People* for repeatedly sharing my mission in the national press, with all the bells and political whistles attached, to keep food poverty on the agenda.

THANK YOU TO SARAH, GEORGI, CAZ, IAN, KEVIN AND ALL OF MY FRIENDS, who have kept my feet on the ground and my eyes looking forward. Thank you for the beer, the understanding and the support every time I wobbled and almost fell. Thank you for telling me I was being an idiot when I was being an idiot, and for laughing at my jokes, and for keeping my press clippings for me, and for being there even when I wasn't.

THANK YOU TO MY DARLING AND DEARLY MISSED GRANDAD, who told me sitting at the Formica table in his guest house that 'those bastards will always try to tell you what to do, and you need to just tell them to piss off'. Thank you for the Le Creuset milk pan, the roll-ups and the laughs.

THANK YOU TO MY DEAR NANNY JOAN, who took me for many a coffee during the book-writing process, and is a rock and a treasure.

THANK YOU TO MY PARENTS, EVELYN AND DAVID, who taught me that a good reputation endures for ever, and who brought me up as a headstrong, independent menace and let me get on with it. As the Dixie Chicks said, we need wide open spaces, room to make our own mistakes. I left school ten years ago with four and a half GCSEs, but I hope that I've made up for that now!

THANK YOU TO JESSICA AND TOMMY, AND YANNIS, DONNA AND ARCHIE, AND ALL OF MY FAMILY.

THANK YOU TO ROBERT GWYN PALMER, CHARLOTTE RIDGE AND ADRIAN SINGTON AT DCD.

THANK YOU TO JOHN HAMILTON, LINDSEY EVANS, TAMSIN ENGLISH, EMMA BROWN AND KATYA SHIPSTER AT PENGUIN for being patient with me every time I exclaimed, 'But I've never written a book! I can't do this!'

THANK YOU TO ROB for standing in my kitchen and cooking my dishes, validating before my eyes that they do actually work and I'm not crazy, that I can make good food and that other people like it.

THANK YOU TO SUSAN for beautiful, beautiful photographs, for the support, and for running with my madcap ideas. Eight o'clock in the morning at the fishing village, anyone?

THANK YOU TO MY READERS – too many to mention – who have kept me strong with words of encouragement, battled Internet trolls on my behalf, cheered me on when I got my book deal and laughed with me, cried with me, reblogged and retweeted me. Thank you to everyone who demanded that I write a recipe book – I hope you're happy with this one and that it's the first of many.

THANK YOU TO MORA AT OXFAM, MOLLY AT THE TRUSSELL TRUST, JONATHON AT JUST FAIR AND EMILY AT CHILD POVERTY ACTION GROUP for extending hands to work together, and for all that you do, and the commitment to all there is left to do.

THANK YOU TO HETTY BOWER, who sadly passed away in November 2013, aged 108. I met Hetty on the campaign trail, spoke with her at the Labour Conference, and she is my hero. A remarkable woman, an inspiring campaigner, and a reminder to never give up fighting for what you believe is right and just and fair. In her own words: 'We may not win by protesting. But if we don't protest we will lose. If we stand up to them, there is always a chance we will win.'